PRAYING AT BURGER KING

Praying at Burger King

Richard J. Mouw

William B. Eerdmans Publishing Company

Grand Rapids, Michigan / Cambridge, U.K.

Published 2007 by
Wm. B. Eerdmans Publishing Co.
2140 Oak Industrial Drive N.E., Grand Rapids, Michigan 49505 /
P.O. Box 163, Cambridge CB3 9PU U.K.

Printed in the United States of America

11 10 09 08 07   7 6 5 4 3 2 1

Library of Congress Cataloging-in-Publication Data

Mouw, Richard J.
Praying at Burger King / Richard J. Mouw.
p.   cm.
ISBN 978-0-8028-4046-2 (pbk.: alk. paper)
1. Christian life — Meditations. 2. Christianity and culture
I. Title.

BV4501.3.M75   2007
248.4 — dc22

2006036406

www.eerdmans.com

Contents

BELIEVING

CHURCH AND WORLD

Preface

When I was appointed to Fuller Seminary's presidency in 1993, I quickly discovered a new genre of speech-making: "a few words from the president." I was expected to greet visiting groups on campus, to open conferences, and to provide brief commentaries for campus publications. These "few-words" exercises could not be lengthy discourses, but neither could they be something as simple as "Welcome! It is good to have you aboard." They had to convey a line of thought that could be developed and completed in a few minutes or a few pages.

Fortunately, I had some practice in coming up with thoughts that could be conveyed in "a few words." For a decade and a half I was actively involved in helping to produce a wonderful little monthly magazine, the *Reformed Journal,* where several us regularly provided short "op-ed" reflections under the heading "As We See It." Since that magazine's demise, I have continued to write similar things in several other journalistic venues — for example, the magazines *Perspectives* and *Christianity Today,* the online sites "Beliefnet" and "On Faith," the blog I recently launched (http://www.netbloghost.com/mouw), and, of course, all of those Fuller-based "few words from the president."

From time to time some folks have urged me to put some of these musings together in a book of short pieces. This little volume is my response to that request. I am grateful to my friend and editor, Jon Pott, for helping me to organize these reflections under some appropriate headings. He and I were members together of the old *Reformed Journal* crowd, and he joins me on this occasion in saluting that gang, especially those who are now writing in a realm where they no longer have to worry about deadlines or word limits.

RJM

LIVING

Praying at Burger King

I pray at Burger King. Bowing to pray in restaurants before I begin eating is a practice I learned in childhood, and I have consciously embraced it as an adult. Sometimes I feel awkward doing so. Sometimes I even decide not to do it — when, for example, I am with folks who might find it a little unsettling after they have started on their salad for me to stop the conversation for a silent prayer. But most of the time when I eat in a restaurant, I bow my head to pray before taking my first bite.

A Christian friend once asked me about it. "Isn't it a bit artificial to do that kind of thing? I mean, sitting in a booth at Burger King, with noisy kids running around — can you really get yourself into a praying mood?"

My answer was that I seldom find myself in a praying mood while sitting in a restaurant. But I typically don't pray because I am feeling especially "spiritual."

If I had to wait for those moods to set in, I wouldn't pray very often! It is precisely because the praying mood doesn't come naturally to me that I make it a habit to pray in restaurants.

My restaurant prayers are opportunities for me to pause and remind myself that there is indeed a God whose mercy reaches out to me even when I am sitting in a fast-food booth with noisy kids running past me. I don't need to be in any special kind of mood to give myself that kind of reminder. In fact, it's generally not a good practice to wait for a certain mood before acknowledging another person's presence. If I am hurrying through a crowded mall and suddenly meet someone I know, I greet the person, even though I haven't had time to get into an especially friendly mood. The person is *there,* and I owe it to her to acknowledge her presence. How much more important to acknowledge God's presence — even in a Burger King.

For me, a larger issue is also at stake. It is an understatement to say that we are living in an increasingly secularized culture. A few decades ago it would not have been uncommon for a restaurant chain to post a "Merry Christmas" or "Happy Easter" sign. How likely would that be today? "Happy Holidays," perhaps, but no explicit reference to a Christian holy day. In our public spaces we are systematically eliminating all reminders of spiritual realities.

I am not enthusiastic about this trend. Still, I do sympathize with some of the reasons why people feel that it is a necessary one. Too often in the past we Christians have abused our privileges here. A Jewish friend told me once how painful it was for him to grow up in a small town where almost everyone else was a member of a Christian church. When the teacher in the public school told the children that it was time, just after the Pledge of Allegiance, "to say the prayer that our Lord Jesus taught," my Jewish friend remained silent. The other kids at school taunted him for this. Some even chanted "Christ killer!" to him in the playground. I am very sorry that happened. That was a terrible way to treat him.

So I do not complain loudly about the campaign to eliminate religious symbols from public spaces. But none of this changes my view of reality. I still believe that wherever we are — whether we acknowledge it or not — we are in the presence of God. There is no distinction between our "private" and "public" lives in God's eyes: "Who can hide in secret places so that I cannot see them? says the LORD. Do I not fill heaven and earth?" (Jeremiah 23:24).

There is no place in all of creation that is outside the scope of God's mercies — not even a Burger King. Cheeseburgers and french fries are, properly understood, gifts from the Lord. The children running past my booth are fashioned in the image of their Creator. Fast-food restaurants are a part of a larger world in which many people are starving. I find it good for my soul to acknowledge these facts. And in making my quiet gesture, I may even be able offer a reminder to the people around me that more is going on in restaurants than meets the secularist eye.

Eye Contact at McDonald's

Listening to a lecture by one of my Fuller Seminary colleagues, a psychologist, I began to feel guilty about the way I had been acting at McDonald's. I came away knowing that I must change my ways.

The professor was Linda Wagener, an expert in adolescent psychology. Several times a year at Fuller we hold a pastors' leadership breakfast on our campus. We want to be in dialogue regularly with people who are out there on the front lines of ministry, and we also want to share with them some of the things we are doing on campus that can enrich their efforts to serve the Lord. This time around I had asked Linda to report on some of her findings about youth culture.

The very idea of a "youth culture," she told us, is a fairly recent phenomenon. It is only in the past several decades that we have come to think of young people as having a "culture" of their very own. To a degree that was unknown in the past, young people these days have their own values, their own sense of group identity, their own ways of dressing and speaking.

This makes life difficult for many families, where parents often do not know how to communicate with their own children. And the opportunities for communication are less frequent than in the past. In many homes, for example, the family dinner — once a daily ritual — is a rare occurrence. We eat on the run, and talk to each other only in passing.

Linda Wagener is doing some important research on teenagers and their families. But she is also deeply concerned about the ways the church ministers to young people. And she worries much about "age segregation." Many congregations these days seem dedicated to keeping young people out of sight of the rest of us. The little kids, for example, are encouraged to leave the "big people's" worship services early on for "children's church." And when they get old enough, they are expected to show up at different times than their parents for their own "youth worship."

Linda does not have easy answers for churches about these practices. But she is firmly convinced that we need to promote direct interaction, both in families and in congregations, between the generations. By keeping our young people out of sight of adults in the life of the church, we are denying the unity of the Body of Christ.

And the fact is that it is not good for either adults or kids to encourage the segregation. Young people are facing difficult and life-changing choices at an early age these days, and they are often doing so with very little guidance or past experience. The values that they choose to live by are often destructive ones. And yet in our church life we often give them the impression that we prefer to keep them out of sight of the older generation.

In her talk, Linda Wagener offered some good suggestions on how to begin to change our patterns. We can think about effective ways in which older and younger generations can find occasions to worship together in a way that encourages the participation of people of all ages. We can strategize about how to get young and old to talk together: Big Brother/Sister programs, mentoring, tutoring — maybe even occasions where kids can teach the older folks how to use computers and video games!

As she was giving her recommendations, she mentioned something about eye contact. And this is where I promised myself to act differently at McDonald's.

We older folks have to stop acting as if we find youth behavior irritating, she said. Kids may act like they don't want interaction with us, but the truth is that they need to be assured that the older generation does take them seriously and cares about them. We can show this in very simple ways, she said. It can happen just by giving a teenager direct eye contact and thanking them for something.

There is an airport McDonald's I stop at often that regularly puts me in a bad mood. The young people who work there are constantly talking to each other and it is hard to get their attention. When it is my turn to order, the young people who serve me often turn sullen. They seldom look me in the eye, and they typically mumble when they speak to me. I respond in an irritated way, and I often shake my head in disgust or raise my eyebrows to communicate my displeasure to whoever is standing in line next to me.

From now on it is going to be different. When I stand in line at that McDonald's, I am going to remember Professor Wagener's lecture. And I am going to silently pray for the kids behind the counter, asking the Lord also to give guidance to all of us who care about effective ministry to young people. And when I get to the head of the line, I am going to ask the person who serves me how he or she is doing, trying my best to make friendly eye contact. And when I receive my Quarter Pounder with cheese, I am going to say "Thank you."

What about Halloween?

Someone remarked recently that Halloween has become our national Mardi Gras. I believe it. You don't have to do much research to conclude that the Halloween season has gotten longer in recent years and that the focus is no longer primarily on children. The costume displays I have been seeing in southern California, beginning already in mid-September, are not dominated by Casper the Ghost outfits for kids and pint-sized witch's hats. Most of this stuff is meant for raucous parties for big people.

I enjoyed Halloween as a kid. And my evangelical parents, not otherwise lax in enforcing standards against "worldly" behaviors, let me enjoy the day. Indeed, they enjoyed it too. As soon as I was able to walk, they dressed me up in a homemade costume and took me door to door collecting treats. They themselves laid in plenty of candy supplies for the neighborhood kids, and they even on occasion turned our basement into a pseudo-horror chamber as a setting for a Halloween party for the church youth group. We knew some evangelical folks, of course, who thought Halloween was "of the devil"; but we considered them to be super-pious killjoys.

There aren't too many things that I am more conservative about than the evangelical generation that raised me, but this is one of them. I still am not a hard-liner on the subject. My grandsons' school puts on a Halloween party, and I don't lose sleep worrying about what is being done to little souls. But evangelicals have been getting stricter on this matter, and I am sympathetic to the trend.

Halloween can be traced to ancient times when some pagans set aside a day to commemorate the end of summer. The spirits of dead people returned to earth at this time, they believed, taking the form of cats and witches and the like. Fearful that these spirits might do them harm, people attempted to scare them away by building fires and displaying pictures of grotesque faces. They would also place food offerings at their doors, in the hope that any visiting spirits would take the treat and forget the trick. Our lighted carved pumpkins, masks, and trick-or-treat rituals have their origins in these practices.

Christians can know all of this and still not automatically be opposed to Halloween celebrations as such. We need to be aware here of what the logicians call "the genetic fallacy" — which occurs when we assume that since something started off with a certain meaning it still has that meaning. Many of our Christian holy days, and the practices associated with them, have pagan origins — but this does not mean that we should not have Christmas trees in our homes or celebrate Easter at a time when the ground begins to "birth" new life.

But should Christians have special worries about Halloween? I think so. At least we ought to be increasingly nervous about Halloween practices in the light of new developments in our culture. When I was growing up, witches and ghosts were things we only read about in children's storybooks. Today, with the re-emergence of Wicca and the new interest in seances and "channeling," they are a very visible religious presence in our culture.

At the very least, this means that Christians cannot view Halloween as just another innocent childhood ritual. For many of our contemporaries it has become, as it was in ancient times, a time to acknowledge the real presence of spiritual forces of good and evil in our lives. For others the yearly event has provided a new excuse to thumb their noses at traditional standards of decency and decorum.

Does this mean no "dress-up" for Christian children? Not necessarily. That needs to be a family decision. But it must *be* a decision. We can no longer take "innocent" Halloweens for granted. At the very least it means that Christian families and churches need to do some serious instructing about what Halloween means to many people. And we must be especially diligent in teaching ourselves and our children that the real antidote to the threat of evil has been provided through the death and resurrection of the One who is the Lord of all of our days and nights.

Surprised by Lent

L ent has never been a natural season of the year for me. I'm not proud of that fact, but it is indeed a fact of my life. I had a lot of Catholic friends as a kid, and Lent was always a big thing for them. They would start talking about Lent already around Valentine's Day (which was a big day in my church year, incidentally, since we evangelicals tended to follow the "Hallmark lectionary" quite closely). They would make the old jokes about giving up watermelon or Ovaltine for Lent, but there was an underlying seriousness about the whole business for them. And then the day would come when they would show up on the school playground with ashes marked on their foreheads. All of this seemed to me a part of a very different kind of religious world than my own.

These days I do try to take Lent seriously. But it isn't easy. Part of the problem is theological in nature. That strand of the Reformed tradition that has shaped my theology has tended, in thinking about the redemptive mission of Jesus, to focus rather intensely on Good Friday, and to some degree on Easter. Jesus came into the world to die on the Cross — and then he was raised from the dead after a few days in the tomb. Everything else was a preface to those main events.

In a theological discussion a few years ago with an Orthodox friend, he made a statement that jarred me. The Incarnation as such, he said — "God being joined to the creation in a new and unique way in Jesus Christ" — this was all by itself a matter of great redemptive significance. The point seemed obvious to him, but it took me by surprise. I found no fault with his comment as I reflected upon it. But it wasn't the kind of thing I was inclined to say.

Why not? Again, the answer is in good part a theological one. The Heidelberg Catechism, one of my reference points for Reformed orthodoxy, says that Jesus delivered us from the torments of hell "by suffering unspeakable anguish and pain, and terror of soul, especially on the cross but also earlier." The "also earlier" clause here comes almost as an afterthought. Of course, he had lived for over three decades prior to Good Friday. And of course this too must be included in the story of his redemptive mission. But the real action took place within the scope of about a week of his life.

I am nevertheless happy that the tradition of Lenten practices forces me to see the larger picture.

The Savior who called out "I thirst" on Calvary had long before cried for his mother's milk in Bethlehem's manger. The agonies of Passion Week were not unconnected to the frustrations and temptations of his adolescent years. The bloody sweat-drops in the garden flowed down the same cheeks as the tears shed at the tomb of Lazarus. "For we do not have a great high priest who is unable to sympathize with our weaknesses" (Hebrews 4:15) — this is a weak claim if we do not recognize the profound ways in which the divine was joined to the creation in the full life of Jesus Christ.

Taking Lent seriously is a lifelong struggle for me. The Lenten season will always catch me off guard — both theologically and in the deeper places of my being. But, given what Lent is all about, that is the way it *should* be. Lent should never fit too easily into the "natural" rhythms of our lives.

Reading Machiavelli

A scholarly journal asked me to review some Machiavellian works: two scholarly commentaries on Niccolo Machiavelli's writings, as well as a new edition of his classic work, *The Prince*. Machiavelli was an Italian political theorist who lived from 1469 to 1527. Back when I was a philosophy teacher who regularly taught courses about political thought, I would think nothing of having a book about or by Machiavelli sitting on my desk. But a seminary president has to be careful about such things. People who come into my office might think that I was reading the book for advice about how to do my job!

I am not a "Machiavellian." We use that label these days to describe people who think that anything goes as long as it works in helping them impose their will on others. Most scholars agree that Machiavelli's own view was not quite that simple. He disliked crude manipulators. The kinds of leaders he admired were a rare commodity, the kind of people who were not content simply to win, but who instead would strive to win nobly. The true "glory" of a good leader, for Machiavelli, was not the attainment of mere pleasure or power but a largeness of spirit that came only with self-discipline and sacrifice.

Machiavelli was especially fond of the military leaders of ancient Rome. They were selfish, but in very complex ways. They possessed the ability, as Machiavelli put it, "to measure [their] forces well." They were bold risk-takers who were not satisfied with small victories. And they also knew that they had to work very hard at creating a public image of themselves as persons who conformed to the long-established patterns of virtue in their communities. The good leader did not have to *be* an honest and caring person. But he did have to *appear* to possess those qualities. At the same time, Machiavelli insisted, good leaders must keep their followers guessing. He even recommended the occasional use of arbitrary executions, so that the followers will not take the leader's benevolent spirit for granted. The successful leader needs to guarantee that people will support him with a touch of fear in their heart, lest they conclude that loyalty to a leader is something that one offers only when it is convenient to do so.

Machiavelli's thought may be more complex than the popular understandings of "Machiavellianism" suggest, but his views are still despicable. His heroes are certainly not the kind of people I want to emulate. In the final analysis, the goals they pursue are soul-destroying. A much nobler view of things is set forth in Max De Pree's books on leadership. Max De Pree, the former CEO of the prestigious Herman Miller furniture company, is a Christian who has thought hard about proper leadership and tried to apply his views to his own corporate leadership. One of his titles by itself points us to a very different perspective than Machiavelli's: *Leading Without Power: Finding Hope in Serving Community*. The attainment of power is not itself the goal of good leadership. Power, the ability to make things happen, must be harnessed to service, a willingness to bring out the best in the people and organizations we help to lead. What leaders should want from their followers is not loyalty rooted in fear, but a deserved trust that is undergirded by a sense of shared purposes. Here the appropriate models are not the military leaders of ancient Rome, but the Savior who was put to death by Roman soldiers on a hill outside of Jerusalem's walls. Jesus did not view his divine power "as something to be exploited, but he emptied himself . . . and became obedient to the point of death — even death on a cross" (Philippians 2:6-8).

To be sure, "servant leadership" can be reduced to platitudes that are not much help in the complexities of life. To "empty ourselves" as leaders does not, for example, mean simply giving people what they think they need. But the servant model can point us to profound ways of thinking about leadership. It calls us to a way of leading in which we are guided, not by visions of self-aggrandizement, but by the qualities of trust, healing, and commitment.

Machiavelli and his disciples have a ready response for those who talk this way. They tell us that we are not "realistic." Ideals are nice things to give speeches about, they say, but they have little practical value. Leaders must regularly choose between the bad and the worse. When "one considers everything well," Machiavelli wrote, "one will find that something that appears a virtue, if followed, would be his ruin, and that some other thing that appears as a vice, if followed, results in his security and well-being."

I agree with Machiavelli that it is important to "consider everything well." Christians, too, are committed to realism. But the "realistic" alternative is the one that best fits with our understanding of reality. And for those of us who accept the Scriptures as our guide to what reality is all about, leaders must be very aware that there is a God who has not left us ignorant about how we are to think and act. The Lord has promised us a wisdom that is to be gained, not by calculating personal costs and benefits, but by praying for the discernment that is available to us if we seek together to do God's will as revealed in the Scriptures.

Good leaders, as Max De Pree puts it, know how to "define reality" and to say "Thank you." The world needs people who are committed to this truly "realistic" way of leading: "and what does the LORD require of you but to do justice, and to love kindness, and to walk humbly with your God?" (Micah 6:8).

The Gift of Integrity

A few years ago my wife and I were driving through northern Minnesota, and in one of the towns that we passed through we noticed that the local Lutheran church was celebrating its centennial. A big sign proclaimed this fact in front of the church building. The sign conveyed this simple message: "One Hundred Years of Grace."

That was a wonderful way of describing that church's presence in that community. They could have chosen some other way to describe their history. For example, they might have emphasized their accomplishments as a congregation in that town, saying something like, "Serving this Community for a Hundred Years," or "A Century of Ministry." Instead, they chose simply to announce to their neighboring community that they saw their presence in that town as a profound sign of God's grace.

Our individual lives are also signs of grace. The

Apostle Paul makes this clear when he tells us, in the opening verses of Romans 5, that our faith in Jesus Christ has given us access to "this grace in which we now stand." It is grace that has saved us, and it is also grace that holds our lives together.

This is important to keep in mind as we attempt to understand what it means to have a Christian character that can sustain us in good times and in bad times. If I had to choose one word that captures the essence of Christian character it would be *integrity*. To have integrity is to be *whole,* in the sense that all of your parts — all of the elements that make you up — are properly in place and working together in a harmonious fashion.

The Bible makes it clear that true integrity is not something we sinful humans can manufacture on our own. It is God's gift to us. In Psalm 41 the psalmist says to the Lord: "In my integrity you uphold me and set me in your presence forever" (v. 12). And he makes it clear that the integrity he is talking about is not something that he has earned on his own. Throughout that psalm he talks about the ways in which the Lord delivers, sustains, and restores him. True integrity comes only from the God who "upholds" us. The Apostle Paul makes the same point when he tells the members of the Philippian church that the God who "began a good work in you will carry it on to completion until the day of Christ Jesus," and that this is possible because "all of you share in God's grace with me"

(Philippians 1:6-7). We sing about this same pattern in the words of that much loved hymn, "Amazing Grace": "'tis grace has brought me safe thus far, and grace will lead me home."

It is all about grace. We human beings are sinners totally incapable of saving ourselves. Salvation can come only from the marvelous grace of God that lifts us out of our depraved condition and restores us to a proper relationship with God through the shed blood of Jesus Christ.

I have to add quickly, however, that in my kind of Calvinist theology there is a dangerous tendency to see ourselves as nothing but helpless and passive creatures who can never take any credit for what we do in our service to the Lord. This would be a mistake. God wants us to be active and to use our unique talents in promoting the work of his Kingdom. As people who have been chosen by sovereign grace to live lives of service to our God, we must respond to this divine initiative by serving the Lord in humility and faithfulness. And central to this life of service is the cultivation of *integrity*.

To cultivate integrity is to work actively at *integrating* our lives. It is to respond to what God has given us in grace by showing forth that integrity in the ways we go about our daily business. We want to demonstrate to others what it is like to be a human being who is "upheld" by God's grace. This integrating activity has to respond to many challenges. We have to learn to hold steady in our Christian character in bad times as well as in good ones. We have to work at being the same person in our very private lives as we are when we are on public display. We have to educate ourselves to see what God is calling us to do in the diverse areas of our lives — as consumers, as citizens, as friends, as family members, as folks who like to be entertained and to exercise and to evangelize and to worship.

All of this can seem an overwhelming assignment. And it certainly is a demanding one. But there is no need to be discouraged. I find a helpful word of guidance from a well-known non-Christian source, the ancient Greek philosopher Socrates. In Plato's dialogue *Meno,* Socrates is depicted as engaging in a very technical conversation with his friends about the nature of virtue. After a number of false starts at defining this notion, his friends are ready to give up. They have a "swarm" of examples of virtue but no coherent understanding of what these examples have in common. Then Socrates gives some helpful advice. Don't get discouraged by the "swarm," he tells them, because, in spite of appearances, "all nature is akin." This means, he says, that there is nothing to hinder us, having learned just one thing, from going on to find out about all of the rest, as long as we do "not weary in seeking."

Socrates is operating with a different worldview than the one the Bible teaches. But he is on to an important point. As Christians, we too believe that "all nature is akin." In Colossians 1 the apostle tells us that in Jesus Christ "all things hold together" (v. 17). The same Lord who the psalmist says is upholding each of us in our integrity is also holding all things in the universe together. So we have even better reasons than Socrates and his disciples had not to be "weary in seeking." We can engage in our efforts — often quite feeble ones, to be sure — to cultivate integrity, knowing that the One who has begun a good work in us will indeed bring it to completeness, to wholeness, on the day of Christ Jesus. This provides us with all the motivation we need to work at living integrated lives.

Greed

We're paying a lot of attention in these days of corporate scandals to greedy people. Not all of this attention is good. For those of us who believe that leadership in the world of corporate business can be an important Christian calling, there is a danger that the present focus on scandalous business behavior will promote cynicism about corporate life, making it difficult to think clearly about the ways in which this area of human activity can be a positive way of serving the Lord. It is crucial, then, that we keep some basics clearly in mind.

The Bible makes it clear that greed is sinful. Greed violates the commandment against covetousness. It is, as the biblical proverb puts it, a life-destroying pattern of behavior (Proverbs 1:19). Having acknowledged the evil character of greed, though, we still need to be clear about what *kind* of evil it is. Some things are intrinsically evil. But others are distortions of something that is good. Greed falls in the latter category.

I am a firm believer in what is sometimes labeled "the Protestant work ethic" — which is a way of referring to a list of virtues that includes such things as thrift, honesty, charity, and a concern for the common good. It also includes *industry,* a commitment to *working hard.* Industrious people are motivated. They want to produce; they crave success; they are eager to turn a profit. There is nothing intrinsically wrong with any of this. Without ambition we would be sluggards.

Here is a way of focusing on an interesting issue. Imagine that Adam and Eve are playing chess together in the Garden of Eden. The Fall has not yet occurred, so there is no sin in their hearts. And yet they still are competing with one another. Each wants to win. But because there is no evil motive at work in their lives, they do not wish each other ill. As healthy competitors they are matching their wits against each other, testing and developing certain skills. This kind of exercise can be an appropriate way to cultivate their created talents.

The world of business is obviously much more complicated than this simple picture. But I am convinced that there, too, competitiveness — ambition, the desire to succeed in productive activity — can function in a healthy way. But as sinners we must be careful to tame these impulses. Industry must be intimately linked to the other virtues — honesty, charity, thrift, a concern for the common good, and the like.

When those links are not maintained, we run the risk of becoming greedy people.

This is what has happened today. The desire to succeed has become disconnected from the cultivation of the other virtues. The task of the Christian community, then, is to call for, and model, lives that are morally and spiritually integrated. Cynicism about corporate leadership as such is not the proper response. What is needed is a renewed emphasis on seeing our daily work as a way to show love both to God and to our neighbors.

Living with Spiritual Awkwardness

The Book of Revelation isn't one of those places we think to go to for humor, but there is a scene right at the end of that book that I do find amusingly touching. As Revelation comes to an end, John has just been given a wonderful vision of the New Jerusalem, with an angel-guide as his companion. John confesses that, having seen and heard all of these marvelous things, "I fell down to worship at the feet of the angel who showed them to me." And the angel immediately admonishes him: "You must not do that! I am a fellow servant. . . . Worship God!" (Revelation 22:8).

Strictly speaking, John's action looks for all the world like idolatry. He is bowing down to someone who is not God. But my hunch is that the reprimand here comes with a twinkle in the angel's eye. John is no idolater. He does not mean to be instituting an angel-worshiping cult. He is just momentarily disoriented. And his confusion is understandable. He has seen a lot of worship going on in his visions. Heavenly choirs have been regularly breaking into songs of praise and elders have been falling down on their faces in adoration. It makes some sense, then, that John, overwhelmed by the glories he has been shown, should drop to his knees in the presence of the nearest celestial citizen. His instinct was to worship, but he aimed his worship in the wrong direction.

I find it comforting that the Holy Spirit would inject this picture of apostolic awkwardness right at the end of the Bible. It is the Lord's way of telling us that he is ever aware of our frailty and finitude, that "he knows how we were made; he remembers that we are dust" (Psalm 103:14).

Very often when I reflect on what I have seen God doing — in my life, in the seminary where I work, in so many other parts of the Kingdom, I am filled with wonder at the riches of God's mercy. The beastly forces of rebellion and destruction are all too obvious in the world. But I have also been privileged to catch a vision of the throne that sits in the heavens, and I have been given the assurance that nothing that happens in the course of history can thwart the good purposes of the One who sits upon that throne. The Lamb has many enemies these days, but he "will conquer them, for he is Lord of lords and King of kings, and those with him are called and chosen and faithful" (Revelation 17:14).

Also like John, I don't have my act together. I continue to be spiritually awkward. I get confused about how to express my sense of wonder. The Lord needs to keep sending me angels to reprimand me. And often those reprimands are given — as they were to John — with a knowing twinkle in the angelic eye.

So I thank the Lord for visions of the glory that he promises to his redeemed people. I also have to admit that we all are spiritually awkward. But I know enough not to let that awareness get me down. The Lord and his angels know the stuff of which we are made!

Asking Questions

Evangelist Tom Skinner once wrote a nice little book with the title *If Christ Is the Answer, Then What Are the Questions?* I have always liked the spirit of that title. We evangelicals have been bold in our proclamation that "Christ is the Answer." But we have not always been good at looking honestly at the questions.

A Fuller alumnus once described for me what he appreciated most about his seminary education. "I came to Fuller with a lot of questions," he said. "I was never allowed to explore them freely at other places where I studied. Fuller gave me a tremendous freedom to work things through in an environment where we were convinced of the truth of the Gospel — but where we were not afraid to ask difficult questions about what the Gospel means for the world in which we live. This experience has made all of the difference in my present ministry!"

Many years ago, when I was deciding on the direction of my academic career, I chose philosophy as my field of specialty because I had many questions that I needed to ask. I still live with questions. One of the things I have discovered — to my delight — as a seminary president is that you can't spend very long talking about "practical" administrative topics — budgets, curriculum, management strategies, educational delivery systems — without rather quickly tapping into basic philosophical questions. What is seminary education all about anyway? How do we measure quality in what we do as a theological institution? How do we best maintain our unity in the midst of diversity?

I have been asking some rather urgent and painful questions of God in recent years — and I know I am not alone in doing so. What is the Lord trying to tell us through the tragic events we regularly witness in our world? How can we best address the fundamental spiritual needs that have come to the surface in the larger world? What do these developments mean for the way we go about our tasks as Christians?

And to tell the truth, I have struggled with even more basic questions. Where *is* God in all of this? How can we go about our "normal" work when our souls are so weighted down by the realities of human suffering? How do I handle my own conflicting feelings — anger, fear, guilt, grief?

In the midst of all of this questioning, I take some encouragement from the fact that the Bible itself is a book of questions. Indeed, there is no question that anyone has asked in recent months that one cannot find in the Psalms. "Why, O Lord, do you stand far off? Why do you hide yourself in times of trouble?" (Psalm 10:1). "How long must I bear pain in my soul, and have sorrow in my heart all day long? How long shall my enemy be exalted over me?" (Psalm 13:2). "For you are the God in whom I take refuge. . . . Why must I walk about mournfully because of the oppression of the enemy?" (Psalm 43:2).

The Bible gives us permission to ask the tough questions. Indeed, no one asked a tougher question than the one the Savior asked on the Cross: "My God, my God, why have you forsaken me?" (Matthew 27:46). And it is precisely because the Son of God asked that soul-wrenching question, that we can have the confidence that our questions ultimately do have answers. That same Lord calls us to obedience to the One who took our questions with him to Calvary, and who offered up those questions out of the depth of his own suffering — and in doing so guaranteed the ultimate victory over sin and death. He is both the Questioner and the Real Answer.

Rules for Prayer Competitors

The couple told me they wished I could provide them with "some theological marriage counseling." I had just finished giving a speech and they had approached the podium area for a brief chat.

"We're only kidding," she said. "Well, *half* kidding," he added, and they smiled at each other. She explained: "He thinks we should go to war against Iraq, and that we should get on with it quickly and get it over with. But I don't think we should fight at all. I favor diplomatic pressure, working through the U.N." He elaborated: "And the problem is that we both pray about this. I pray for war and she prays against it. When you mentioned the Civil War movie, you touched on a sensitive nerve for us."

In my talk I had referred to *Gods and Generals*, a film that focuses on the way in which two Southern generals, Robert E. Lee and Stonewall Jackson, defended their cause by appealing to Scripture and praying for a divine blessing on their efforts. Many Christians in the North, I observed, prayed with equal fervor that the South would be defeated. And this isn't just a piece of past history, I said. "Competing prayers" happen all the time — especially right now, as Christians line up on both sides of the debates about Iraq.

I don't blame the couple who talked to me for expressing frustration about their competing prayers. It is one thing for married folks to prefer different candidates in a local election. If my wife thinks that I am supporting the wrong person for political office, she can at least take comfort in knowing that her vote cancels out mine. But when it comes to prayer, there is no cancelling out. When we talk to God, we are not casting votes. When we offer up competing prayers in a warfare situation, we are hoping that the Ruler of the Universe will take sides. And that means that one of us is asking God to do the wrong thing.

I don't have the answers to all of the questions that can be raised about competing prayers. I am as tempted as anyone else to want God to see it my way. But I do think there are a few rules we can try to follow in our prayer-competitions.

Keep praying about what matters to you. Don't let the awareness that someone else is praying for the opposite cause intimidate you from praying about what is on your heart. God knows we are finite beings with limited perspectives on what is happening in the world. What he wants from us is that we acknowledge our dependence upon him. This means that it pleases the Lord when we talk to him about what is on our hearts and minds, even if we show our biases in doing so.

Focus on the underlying issues. Rather than telling God what to do, concentrate on your underlying hopes and fears. Explain to God what you are most worried about, and express your hopes about how things might turn out. Rather than requesting a specific outcome — "Give our side the victory!" — ask for things like insight, wisdom, courage, patience, both for yourself and for the decision-makers.

Pray for those whom you consider to be your enemies. This mandate comes directly from Jesus: "Love your enemies and pray for those who persecute you" (Matthew 5:44). We can't give up on anyone to whom God gives a chance to repent and change their ways.

Acknowledge that you might be wrong in the way you view things. I like the way the writer of Psalm 139 does this. At one point he gets quite excited about the fact that he and God are on the same side: "Do I not hate those who hate you, O LORD? And do I not loathe those who rise up against you? I hate them with a perfect hatred; I count them my enemies" (vv. 21-22). But then he seems to pause and take stock. (I imagine him saying "Oops!" at this point.) His mood changes: "Search *me*, O God, and know *my* heart; test *me* and know *my* thoughts. See if there is any wicked way in *me*, and lead *me* in the way everlasting" (vv. 23-24).

If I ever go into business as a theological marital therapist, I think I will encourage couples who are engaging in prayer competitions to say Psalm 139 together at least once each day!

A Missionary Calling

As a child I regularly attended services that would conclude with the preacher's urging us — with "every head bowed and every eye closed" — to consider whether the Lord was calling us to "full-time Christian service." At one of those services I raised my hand and promised the Lord that I would be a missionary when I grew up. I remember vividly what I had in mind: I saw myself laboring in some jungle village somewhere, leading people to Jesus.

I did not end up in a jungle. And I have from time to time felt a twinge of guilt about the fact that my life has gone in a very different direction than what I envisioned in that early moment of spiritual intensity. Not that I think the Lord holds us to all of the promises made in our childhood. But I have on occasion wondered whether I chose a path that was too easy to walk. I have spent over thirty years now pursuing "full-time service" in Christian higher education, and I really cannot imagine a line of work that I could have enjoyed more. On the other hand, I know that the enjoyable path is not necessarily the wrong one. Many good Christian people would be miserable reading the books that I read and thinking the thoughts that I think. God not only calls us to walk in certain paths; he also creates in us the disposition to like some of the things he calls us to do.

Lately, though, I have been thinking that maybe, in a way, I kept my childhood promise after all. Those of us who hang around in theological circles are aware these days — or at least we ought to be — that we in North America are living in a "post-Christian" culture. We are surrounded by superstitions, some ancient, some newly crafted. The pagan thoughts and practices that were once thought to find their home only in "foreign lands" now flourish in our own neighborhoods. We don't have to search very long in North America to find most of the beliefs and practices that I once imagined I would encounter only in a rain forest! As some theologians have been insisting lately, the northern hemisphere church is in a "missionary location."

In those services of my childhood we sang hymns that emphasized total surrender to the will of God. One of those songs expressed the conviction that "if by a still small voice he calls/to paths that I do not know,/ I'll answer, 'Dear Lord, with my hand in Thine/I'll go where you want me to go.'" I must say that in my daily work I constantly have to start walking on "paths that I do not know." These are strange and troubling days, in which human beings — whatever the continent on which they live their lives — face new confusions and dilemmas. Many of the old guideposts are no longer visible. The maps we have long relied upon now need to be redrawn. Like the missionaries of the past, we all may find ourselves traveling in uncharted territories.

We can learn much from the missionaries of former days. They stepped out in faith with the conviction that there was nowhere they could go on this planet that was not under the rule of the One to whom all authority has been given: "The earth is the LORD's and the fulness thereof, the world and all who dwell therein" (Psalm 24:1). They knew that he owns the cattle on a thousand hills, and that they would never meet a human being in any rain forest or desert oasis who was not created in the image of the God who sent Jesus into the world.

We are missionaries all. Whatever our daily work as Christians, we can face the future in the confidence that the One who calls us to serve his cause will also send his Spirit to guide us on the way. Indeed, he *is* the Way!

Housecleaning and "Visualization"

We were strolling through a mountain village in Colorado when I came across a handbill advertising a local housecleaning service. This particular company offered to do much more than a mere scrubbing and dusting. They promised to help any homeowners to "visualize the ideal state of your house and align your house with its highest potential."

Obviously a New Age approach to housecleaning. And I know some evangelical writers who would insist that this is no innocent matter. One prominent critic of the New Age movement has branded all "visualization" activities as occult. He criticized Robert Schuller, for one, because Schuller encourages people who are about to have a job interview to spend some time before the interview visualizing a successful outcome. This is shamanism, said the critic. It is based on a "mind-over-matter" philosophy.

My own response to the critic is to suggest that he

lighten up a bit. Not all "visualizations" should be identified as occult. Indeed, "visualizing" ideal outcomes can be an act of faith — a way of strengthening one's trust in God's promises. The writer to the Hebrews says, at the beginning of the great "faith chapter" in that epistle, that "faith is the substance of things hoped for, the evidence of things unseen" (Hebrews 11:1). With the eyes of faith we can grasp something of the future that God has in store for us and gain the strength to move toward that future.

I have no problems applying this even to housekeeping. Suppose a Christian couple has for a long time lived in a very messy home. Things have gotten so out of hand that they are too discouraged to begin correcting their ways. The fact is, though, that if they would simply take some first steps, and then keep at the project for a while, they could do much to improve their living conditions. They might be greatly helped by a company — even a New Age company — that came alongside them, helping them to "visualize the ideal state" of their living space, aligning it with "its highest potential." Whatever their New Age consultants might have in mind, such an exercise can be for them a genuine act of trusting that the Lord will strengthen them to be better stewards of the resources that God has made available to them.

Our personal "visualization" endeavors are exercises in faith — but they should not require a blind faith. They call for a faith that is shaped by a discerning vision of what is possible in God's scheme of things. To reflect on our goals, to look ahead with the eyes of faith — this can be a God-honoring "visualization," a responsible Christian exercise of a faith that "is the substance of things hoped for, the evidence of things unseen." As believers who know that our supreme task in life is to glorify the Lord, we may even be able to demonstrate to our New Age friends and neighbors what it *really* means to visualize an ideal state of affairs and to align ourselves — both individually and collectively — with our highest potential!

Thinking about Work

R ed-eye flights are becoming more popular, according to recent surveys. There was a time not long ago when a passenger boarding a late night coast-to-coast flight could expect to stretch out over three seats in the coach section. Not so these days. Many night-time flights are solidly booked. The newspaper story suggests that this phenomenon has something to do with changing attitudes toward work in our "new economy." One internet manager is quoted as saying that he takes all-night transcontinental flights because it lets him work full days without having to "blow a whole day traveling."

There may be something about the high-tech culture that promotes this kind of thing, but much of it strikes me as plain old-fashioned drivenness. I know the feeling. In a few weeks I will leave a day of meetings in Southern California to fly all night to Charlotte, North Carolina, for a conference that begins first thing in the morning. I took on both of these assignments knowing full well that only a red-eye flight would let me do them. The trustees who monitor my presidential patterns tell me not to do this kind of thing. But I sometimes ignore their (and my wife's) advice because of what I see as important parts of "my work."

Labor Day is a good time to think about the patterns of our working lives. Ostensibly it is a day set apart to celebrate the central importance of work for our collective existence. But for those of us who are caught up in the demands of "our work," it is important that we devote some time for serious reflection about what work means in our contemporary culture.

In my younger days as a Christian ethicist, I was convinced that the most important thing to preach about our working lives was this: *Work is more than an economic activity.* I still think that is an important piece of guidance. But most of the driven people that I know do not seem to be motivated primarily by the desire to make money. Indeed, pastors who counsel "new-economy" types tell me that many of these people feel awkward about their newly gained wealth. They don't want to adopt ostentatious lifestyles. They are interested in giving money to good causes. What keeps them going is not the profit-motive, but creative impulses and a fascination with risk-taking.

What many of us need these days is to reflect regularly on a much broader maxim: *Life is more than work.* This is really what the biblical sabbath is all about. Keeping regular days of rest is not an arbitrary divine mandate. God himself rested after six days of divine "labor" in creating the world. Work is an important part of what the Creator meant for us to be and do. But we weren't designed to have it permeate all of our lives. Play, sleep, relaxed conversation, courtship, the marital bedroom, cultivating friendships, simply "wasting time" — all of these are important elements in the rhythms of healthy living. This emphasis on integrated living is actually at the heart of "the Protestant ethic," even though that pattern has often been seen as responsible for much of our drivenness — and even though the teaching is central to Catholic and Jewish views of the good life as well.

A number of social commentators in recent years have insisted that democracy and capitalism, while very good things in their accounts of healthy human existence, are not self-sustaining. Each of them — and "democratic capitalism," the combination of the two — will ultimately self-destruct if not undergirded by a value-system that features the importance of character, good-will, honesty, thrift, charity, and the like. These virtues are sadly lacking in many of the countries that are now embracing the free market after a long and debilitating obsession with Marxism. Those of us who live in cultures where democracy and capitalism have flourished have an obligation to export, not only our political and economic theories, but the values and worldviews that are necessary to sustain the good life. We cannot export that which we ourselves do not possess in abundance. Labor Day is one of the times when we can begin to put things into perspective again.

Letting Chickens Strut Their Stuff

S ome Christian friends were talking about the debates that are raging these days about "animal rights," and they left no room for doubt about what side they were on. They wanted nothing to do with the folks who protest fur coats. And they certainly had no sympathy for the viewpoint — made popular by a well-known ethicist — that the life of a healthy dog may be more valuable under circumstances than that of a sick child.

I have no real disagreement with these friends on the basic issues. But I tend to hold back a little bit when Christian people make light of animal rights. I keep remembering a lesson that a devout chicken farmer taught me many years ago.

On the face of it, the lesson does not seem to come to much. "Chickens are chickens," he said. But in the context in which he made his point, it struck me as a profound truth.

I was a graduate student at the time, and I was digging deep into questions about ethics and social policy.

In a church bulletin I noticed that some Christian farmers were getting together to discuss the relationship between their faith and their farming practices, and I decided to listen in. It was an intriguing session. These folks — most of them Mennonite and Dutch Reformed — were serious about their religion and they wanted their deepest convictions to make a difference in the way they lived their daily lives.

It was obvious that the chicken farmer had spent many hours working outdoors. His face was heavily tanned up to that point on his brow where his hat protected his bald head from the sun. He had a strong Dutch accent, and my guess was that he had not received much formal education. But he was in his own way eloquent, especially on the subject of a mass-production approach to chicken farming. "Colonel Sanders wants us to think of chickens only in terms of dollars and cents," he announced. "They are nothing but little pieces of meat to be bought and sold for food. And so we're supposed to crowd them together in small spaces and get them fat enough to be killed." And then he moved toward his theological lesson: "But that's wrong! The Bible says that God created every animal 'after its own kind.' Chickens aren't people, but neither are they nothing but hunks of meat. Chickens are chickens and they deserve to be treated like chickens! This means that we have to give each chicken the space to strut its stuff in front of other chickens."

This farmer was no vegetarian. And I'm pretty

sure that most of his chickens ended up on people's dinner tables. But he also sensed an obligation to treat his chickens with dignity — not human dignity, mind you, but chicken dignity.

My guess is that he would not have been able to answer all of the tough questions we might pose to him about the rights and wrongs of raising chickens. But, then, the sophisticated secularist defenders of animal rights these days don't have all the details worked out either. This is not an area where consistency on all points comes easily.

My chicken farmer was setting forth some practical spiritual wisdom. As harsh as it may seem to the all-life-is-equal folks these days, from a biblical perspective there is indeed a kind of hierarchy of life. Read Psalm 8. God is "higher" and we humans are "lower" — but not as "low" as the animals.

God tells human beings to exercise "dominion" over the rest of creation (Genesis 1:28). But that does not give us a right to do anything we want with nonhuman life. Dominion is not the same as domination. The old-fashioned term is that we have been made "stewards" of the world that God made. We are caretakers. This means we must *take care* in the way we treat the animals. The farmer was right when he insisted that the fact that there are different "kinds" means that we must allow for different kinds of *dignity*. Chickens are chickens, after all. So, even if we are raising them for profit, we still need to give them room to strut their stuff!

"Christian Stuff"

Shortly after I set off from my hotel on an early morning run, I saw a storefront bearing the intriguing inscription, "Brother Ray's Christian Stuff." I stopped jogging to see what time the store would open that morning, only to read the disappointing message that Brother Ray was on vacation for a few weeks. Pressing my face to the glass, however, I was able to discern that Brother Ray had a rather expansive understanding of what kind of stuff can properly be called Christian.

My sentiments are with Brother Ray: the more things we can claim for Christ the better. One of my spiritual heroes, the great nineteenth-century Dutch statesman Abraham Kuyper, put it exactly right: "There is not a square inch in the whole domain of our human existence," he wrote, "over which Christ, who is Sovereign over *all,* does not cry: "Mine!" Kuyper was expounding on an important biblical theme: "The earth is the LORD's, and all that is in it, the world and all who live in it" (Psalm 24:1). A very broad definition of "Christian stuff"!

The temptation, of course, is to place limits on what belongs to the Lord. Sometimes this reductionistic tendency is due to a sloppy way of putting things. A college student once said to me: "I have been doing nothing for several months but study, study, study! I have been so wrapped up with books that I haven't had any time for the things of the Lord."

I knew what he meant. The life of the scholar — student or teacher — can be demanding. Deadlines and more deadlines. As soon as one three-hour exam is over, you have to start worrying about the twenty-page paper that is due — or needs to be graded — in two weeks. At times "study, study, study" can be more than a human being can handle.

But for all of my sympathy, I still worry when I hear students or teachers draw a stark contrast between academic pursuits and "the things of the Lord." After all, I would say, the demands of school are themselves "the things of the Lord." If I could rewrite the student's complaint for him in proper theological terms, I would put it this way: "I have been so wrapped up with books that I haven't had any time for some of the *other* things of the Lord."

Jesus is Lord over books, term papers, quizzes, laptops, dissertations, and class discussions. He is Lord over all of the other "stuff" in our lives as well.

He is the Lord of these things even when his Lordship is not acknowledged. When a group of professed atheists write learned papers about topics in molecular biology, they are dealing with "the things of the Lord," even if they refuse to acknowledge the fact that their very minds, the paper they write on, the cells that they study, the electricity that powers their computers — all these things were created by God and were designed to bring him glory and honor.

I preach a lot about the importance of academic "stuff." The things of the classroom are indeed the things of the Lord. But I need constant reminders that the other dimensions of life are also important to the Lord. My student friend was right to recognize the need for praying and singing hymns and sharing testimonies and walking in the woods. God wants us to engage in these kinds of things, because they also have to do with "stuff" that belongs to him.

Doing Something "Religious"

There's an old joke I have heard many times. It comes in different versions, but the basic plot is always the same. A group of people are in difficult circumstances and someone decides that the situation is bad enough that the time has come to "do something religious." Someone finds a receptacle and passes it around as a collection plate.

I see the humor. Some religious leaders and organizations seem especially interested in getting our money. We hear it often from the televangelists, for example: "We need your gifts. If this important program is to continue to bring the truth to an unbelieving world, it is urgent that you call the number on your screen. Have your credit card ready. And be sure to ask for your free copy of. . . ."

But I have been impressed in the past few years by some more profound "do something religious" impulses. Obviously, a lot of such impulses got played out in the wake of 9/11. But I also saw them at work later when the Columbia spacecraft was destroyed during its descent. When we first heard the reports of that terrible accident, we were shocked and dismayed. It soon became clear, though, that many people were not content simply to grieve quietly. They needed to *do* something. And the something that they did was often very religious. There were, of course, the obvious things. Churches, temples, and synagogues held services, and people turned out in large numbers. The president addressed the nation and quoted a moving passage from the prophet Isaiah. Flags were lowered to half-mast to honor those who had died.

But there were other things as well. People who lived within several hours' driving distance of the Florida space center drove there to stand together and pray. In various communities citizens placed flowers or some other symbol at an appropriate place. In areas of Texas where pieces of debris from the spacecraft had fallen, people gathered silently to gaze upon the fragments.

I'm not sure that all of the people who did these things were aware of the connections, but what they were engaging in were contemporary expressions of ancient rituals. Pilgrimages to sacred places. The creation of local shrines. Venerating sacred relics. Indeed, the very language we used to honor the space travelers who died came close to viewing them as saints and martyrs.

Many of my fellow evangelicals would not be pleased about these patterns. We have long been suspicious of anything that felt too "Catholic" — or worse yet, too pagan. But I think we should look at these ways of "doing something religious" in a positive light.

I would want to argue the same way in support of the interreligious gatherings that were held shortly after 9/11. On those occasions, too, important spiritual impulses were at work. And however we might rightly puzzle over how to understand such events theologically, my own sense is that we cannot simply dismiss those gatherings as nothing more than "generic religiosity."

At Fuller Seminary we are dealing with issues that have direct relevance to what is happening in our world. Many people in North America may be spiritually confused these days — but it is indeed a *spiritual* confusion. It has become clear in recent times of crisis that human beings instinctively search for answers to some very basic questions: Where can we find true safety? How can we live our lives in a world in which we are surrounded by danger? What are the things that really count as we face an uncertain future?

Those questions are even closer to the surface in other parts of the world. Suicide bombings. The ravages of warfare. The AIDS epidemic. Political and economic turmoil. Natural catastrophes.

There is only one safe place in the whole universe, and that is "in the shelter of the Most High, . . . in the shadow of the Almighty" (Psalm 91:1). Of course, those of us who have found that safe place have no business keeping the secret to ourselves. Other people are searching for what we have found. To point the way for them is, in the best sense, "doing something religious"!

BELIEVING

Large Vision, Steady Focus

"To see life steadily and see it whole." This line from the great nineteenth-century British writer Matthew Arnold was quoted frequently by my college teachers to describe the basic goal of a liberal arts education. I can't recall coming across this line anywhere in recent years, though. Part of the reason is that Arnold himself seems to have fallen out of style — the experts no longer point to his writings as a model of excellence in literature. But the actual conviction expressed in that one line is also not very popular these days. When folks these days talk in lofty terms about higher education — when they rise above, for example, descriptions of the marketability of a specific course of study — they are more likely to wax eloquent about the benefits of "critical thinking."

Don't get me wrong — I am all in favor of critical thinking. My academic training is in philosophy and I have spent a good part of my career encouraging students to engage in critical reflection on the things that most people simply take for granted. I remember many years ago coming across a wonderful line from Anglican preacher John Stott, addressed to those of us involved in evangelical social action. We all need to be "conservative radicals," he said. We need to be conservative about one thing, and one thing alone: the absolute authority of God's Word. And on the basis of taking that authority with utmost seriousness, we need to be willing to call every other assumption into question.

John Stott had it right. But I am sure he was not meaning to give the impression that an unrelenting questioning of everything is the goal of the Christian life. No, the goal is obedience to the will of God as revealed in the Scriptures. That's how I see the goal of seminary education. We learn critical thinking in order better to serve the Lord. We are in the business of attempting to get clearer in our hearts and minds about the basic issues of life in order more effectively to promote the cause of the Gospel of Jesus Christ. The Lutheran theologian Robert Jenson put it nicely in something I read recently. Christian teachers need to remember, he said, that in our understanding of the faith we start with "I believe . . . ," and not with "I wonder about. . . ."

Matthew Arnold's line — "to see life steadily and see it whole" — fits nicely with the goal of trying to spell out the "I believe" for a life of obedience to our Lord. We live in a world in which people's lives are increasingly fragmented. We need to point them — by the example of our own lives — to the big picture: the all-encompassing Kingdom of Jesus Christ, the divine Reign administered by the One to whom all authority in heaven and on earth has been given. That provides us with a large vision and a steady focus.

Entrenched?

S he was writing a news story on the debates over "same-sex unions" in the mainline churches, and she needed a few lines from an evangelical on the subject. I think she was fighting a deadline — she seemed in a bit of a hurry. I, too, was having a busy day, and I had no desire to make the interview go longer than necessary. But when she used the word "entrenched" I knew I had to slow things down a bit.

Here is how it came up. She was describing some things that the Protestant defenders of "same-sex unions" were saying, and she regularly referred to their views as "progressive." Then she asked me for my response: "So, what would you say from a more . . . um . . . how shall I say it — a more *entrenched* position?" At that point I insisted that we talk a little about labeling systems before I was willing to give her the comment she needed.

I can understand how she could come up with the

"entrenched" label. Earlier, she had used the word "conservative" to describe people like me, and I had not protested. When you admit that you want to "conserve" some things from the past, it is not silly for someone to think that you are one of those people who digs a trench and attempts to hold the ground at all costs. So "entrenched" is not so far-fetched a term. But I still do not like the label very much.

The ironic thing was that only a few days earlier another journalist was interviewing me about new patterns of worship. Many evangelicals are sponsoring "seeker-sensitive" church services these days, where many of the traditional forms of worship have been replaced by rock bands, "praise choruses," dramatic skits, and sermons delivered by pastors wearing blue jeans and tee-shirts. In this interview I was the one who was saying good things about change, about trying new things. And it just so happened that my views about worship were being contrasted with the views of many of the same folks who defend "same-sex unions" — except that when it came to questions about worship, they were the ones who were resisting change. But the reporter who was writing about worship did not think to describe those leaders as "entrenched."

So to the degree that the "entrenched" label does apply to people like me, it also applies to the folks that we disagree with on important matters. If it is fair to say that *some* of us dig trenches, then we should be clear about the fact that we *all* do it — and we all do it selectively. For example, some Protestants want to relegate the ancient creeds of the church to theological museums; others of us want to conserve them as living testimonies. You might want to describe us as entrenched on this subject. When we get into an argument with many of those same Christians about abortion-on-demand, though, some of us want to set aside "Roe versus Wade" while the pro-choicers start digging their own trenches. And we can multiply examples. The "left" wants to conserve affirmative action policies; the "right" wants to progress beyond these practices. But the "right" digs trenches in defending prayer in the public schools, while the "left" sees religious neutrality as a sign of progress. And so on. No one simply wants to "progress," no matter what the particular cause is. Nor does any of us really want to be on the "conserving" side of every argument about whether or not to change.

All of this makes me wonder whether it would not be better to rely on some different metaphors in our attempts to sort out the ways in which we disagree on important subjects. Trench-digging is a rather militant activity. The biblical writers provide an alternative picture in emphasizing the notion of a journey. The Psalms especially make much of this theme: to be a proper worshipper of God is to walk a certain kind of path, it is to follow a special "way." Here is a nice example from Psalm 119: "I run the way of your commandments, for you enlarge my understanding."

Each of us is on a journey through life. It is important, biblically speaking, that we find the right "way." In this context, it is not a good thing to dig too many trenches. It may be necessary, of course, to engage in a battle on occasion — I do not want to rule out the realities of "culture wars." But these divert us from the important business of moving along on the "way" we have chosen. And we should be clear about the fact that we do choose the paths that we walk. To encourage same-sex unions and abortion-on-demand is to walk a different "way" than to discourage such things.

We need to talk about our choice of paths. To do so is to point to the markers that we follow along our way. It is to compare our maps and to assess the directions in which our choices lead us. Dialogue about these matters is of great importance. It is even good and necessary to argue about such things. But we can do so by walking together for a while, talking as we go. In that sense we can all be "progressive." And we can avoid digging too many trenches.

"It's OK!"

It happened over a half century ago, but I still remember clearly the day that Santa Claus came to our kindergarten class. In scheduling Santa's surprise visit, the teacher must have thought it would be a treat for all of us. What stands out in my memory, though, is the fright it gave me when he came shouting through the door. But every year during the Christmas season I also remember a whispered message of comfort I received from that same Santa on that day long ago.

Our teacher had arranged for Santa to make a dramatic entry during an afternoon early in the Christmas season. We were all sitting at our desks doing our kindergarten thing, when suddenly the door burst open and in came a large bearded man in a red suit with white trimming. "Ho, ho, ho, boys and girls!" He continued to shout: "I'm here to find out who has been naughty and nice this year!" I was terrified, and I was aware of the fear that my class-mates also felt.

Santa sat in the chair that the teacher offered him in front of the class. Again he spoke in what seemed to my five-year-old ears like a thundering voice: "I would like you children to take turns sitting on my lap, and I'm going to ask you questions about what you would like for Christmas this year! And I want to check to see whether you deserve to receive any presents at all! Who will be first?"

Santa scanned the room. None of us made a move. Finally, he pointed his finger straight at me. "That young man there. Come up here and sit on my lap." I was frozen to my seat, but Santa coaxed me forward. Reluctantly, I made my way to his chair. Santa took hold of me with strong hands and placed me on his lap. He could not help but feel my trembling body.

Then an important thing happened. The person playing the role of Santa that day, it turned out, was a man from our church, Mr. Cooper. I knew him well, al-though I did not recognize him in his disguise. Sensing my fright, Santa whispered in my ear, in a gen-tle voice that only I could hear: "Richard! It's OK. It's me. Mr. Cooper. Don't be afraid." As soon as I figured out what was going on, I relaxed. I was able to answer Santa's questions. His voice took on a much kinder, re-assuring tone for the rest of his visit. And when it was clear that I could handle my encounter with Santa Claus, the rest of the class seemed to relax as well.

I think about that encounter with Santa every Christmas season. As I have gotten older it has become clear to me that he was an important bearer of the Christmas message for me that day in the kindergarten classroom. "Don't be afraid," he told me.

Whether Mr. Cooper realized it or not, when he whispered those words to me he was expressing a major theme in the Bible's account of the events leading up to the birth of Jesus. Mary was frightened when the angel came to tell her she would become pregnant, and the angel said to her, "Do not be afraid." The angel also visited Joseph to encourage him to marry his pregnant fiancée: "Do not be afraid," the heavenly messenger said to him.

And then there was that wonderful night when the shepherds suddenly were surrounded by the bright light of God's glory as an angel appeared to them. "And they were terrified," the Gospel writer tells us. But the angel spoke these words again: "Do not be afraid; for see — I am bringing you good news of great joy for all people: to you is born this day in the city of David a Savior, who is the Messiah, the Lord."

This year once again I need to hear the words that Mr. Cooper spoke to me as a child — words that are also the message of the Christmas angels. "Do not be afraid." I always knew in an intellectual way that people in many parts of the world live in daily fear of death and mass destruction. But those fears have now come very close to home for me — and for all of us who live in North America and other "advanced" societies. Our buildings, our planes, our military fortresses — none of these feel as safe as they did only a few years ago.

I am glad, then, that we can celebrate Christmas again. As a Christian I need to hear the message once more. And while that message says things that I have heard many times before, some words will come to me this year with new meaning and as a new source of comfort. "Do not be afraid." I'm thankful to Mr. Cooper for whispering that message to a frightened child. But I am even more thankful that God sent the angels to say those words to people long ago — and to all of us today who see the birth of the baby Jesus as the most significant event in all of history.

The Christmas story tells me that the vulnerable baby who lay in the manger is "God with us." God knows what it is like to be afraid. And when God's messengers tell me that I do not have to be afraid anymore in the deep places of my being, I can get on with the important task of living the life that God wants me to live.

Good News for the Sheep

I wish I knew more about how the sheep acted on that first Christmas night when the angels visited the shepherds. I found out awhile back that I come from a long line of Dutch shepherds. Maybe that explains why sheep, and especially lambs, have always been my favorite animals.

I had an interesting encounter with a lamb a few years ago when my wife and I were in Holland. We were driving around the back roads of my ancestral region one afternoon in April. That time of year is a great time for observing sheep because there are a lot of lambs, and lambs are marvelous creatures to watch. My wife has a delightful image that nicely captures what they do. She says they are "spring-loaded." You will often see a lamb standing still and then all of a sudden it leaps into the air and it frolics its way across the pasture.

When we came upon a particularly pleasant field

full of sheep, we pulled over to the side of the road, and I went over to the fence with a camera to photograph some lambs. Suddenly one little lamb leaped into the air — spring-loaded — and came running right up to the fence. It came to a quick stop and looked at me, cocking its head.

In that moment I had a strange experience. It felt like we actually recognized each other, that lamb and I. For a few brief seconds I wondered whether maybe this lamb might be a descendent of some sixteenth-century sheep who had been shepherded by some sixteenth-century ancestor of mine. The lamb was looking straight at me; we had eye contact. And it was as if the lamb was saying, "Should I know you?"

I always think about that lamb now when I hear the story about the Christmas shepherds. Here is how I now picture things in my imagination. While the shepherds were sore afraid as they listened to the angels, one little lamb frolicked to a place where it could get a good view of what was going on. Then it cocked its head, looking up at the angels — just like the Dutch lamb looked at me — with a look in its eyes that said, "Is something special happening here?"

My little fantasy does have a theological point. From a biblical perspective, lambs had a lot riding on what happened on that first Christmas night. We all know that lambs frolic a lot, but in reality, ever since the Garden of Eden, they have had a fairly miserable existence. Right around the time when Adam and Eve ate the forbidden fruit, I expect that there was a lamb, not too far away in the Garden, who was cuddled up against a wolf. All was going well, as usual, between the wolf and the lamb, and the lamb was feeling very secure. Then suddenly the wolf stirred like it had never stirred before and the lamb noticed a strange look in the wolf's eye. For the first time in its life, the lamb felt a primal fear fill its whole being. And then the lamb gave in to a strange new instinct: terrorized, it began to run away. Quickly, the wolf growled and began to chase the lamb. And ever since, wolves have been chasing lambs.

Yes, lambs had a lot riding on what happened that night in Bethlehem. The child whose birth was announced by the angels had been long awaited by lambs. This baby was coming into the world to undo the bad things that had happened long ago in the Garden. Because of what this child would accomplish, there would come a day when lambs would cuddle up against wolves again, and feel safe.

Lambs had a lot riding on what happened in Bethlehem that night — but not just because of what it meant for their relationships with wolves. The birth of the child also meant something about how lambs and human beings would get along. After what happened in the Garden, lambs would have a very central and unfortunate role in the business of making sacrifices for atonement: people slaughtered lambs as a way of attempting to pay for their sins. But because of the baby who was being born on Christmas night, the time had arrived when never again would lambs have to be offered on the altars of sacrifice. One day soon this baby would grow up and his cousin would look at him and proclaim in a loud and authoritative voice: "Behold, the Lamb of God that takes away the sins of the world."

Lambs had a lot riding on what happened that night. But there was even more at stake for human beings. When the Bible talks about what it means for us that the Savior was born in Bethlehem, it also uses sheep imagery. The child who was born would feed his flock like a shepherd; he would gather the little lambs and hold them close to his bosom, gently leading those who are with young. Even more significantly: "All we like sheep have gone astray; we have all turned to our own way, and the LORD has laid on him the iniquity of us all" (Isaiah 53:6).

The first Christmas night was an important night for the lambs. But it was even more important for us.

He Did *Weep*

Christmas hymns are among my favorite music. There is one line, though, in "Away in a manger" that bothers me theologically: "But little Lord Jesus no crying he makes."

I believe with all my heart that Jesus cried in the manger. There was no little Superman suit hidden under those swaddling clothes. The little Lord Jesus wasn't lying there thinking about the angels and anticipating the scheduled visit of the shepherds. He was a very real baby with the needs and frustrations that all real babies have. What was written of him as an adult, in that shortest of all Bible verses, could also have been said of him as a baby: "Jesus wept" (John 11:35). He wept as a child because he came to suffer in all the ways that we suffer, including the ways in which newborn babies suffer. We often refer to the week in which the crucifixion took place as "Passion Week," but the passion of Jesus — his taking our frailty upon himself —

was already happening during his first week of life on earth.

Some Christian writers of the past spent a lot of time reflecting on the ways Bethlehem and Calvary were alike, and they were quite imaginative in coming up with parallels. Mary knelt at his cradle and at his cross. Jesus cried for his mother's milk in the manger and he cried out "I thirst" on Calvary. The magi brought him precious ointments in his infancy and his friends anointed him with myrrh for his burial. Both the stable and the tomb were borrowed. Swaddling clothes and funeral garments. And so on.

Such thoughts — traditionally associated with what was called "the Devotion to the Infant Jesus" — can have a morbid feel to them. We also need to think about the risen and ascended Lord when we see the baby Jesus. Bethlehem is, in the words of another carol, "the dawn of redeeming grace." The angels who told the shepherds of his birth also sing praises to the Savior who now sits on heaven's throne. Already in the manger "God was in Christ reconciling the world unto himself" (2 Corinthians 5:19). Bethlehem's baby was on his way to victory!

But the One who now sits in glory on the throne did become in Bethlehem like one of us. And because the Savior cried in the manger and thirsted on the cross, we can proclaim the wonderful message of the love that brought the Son of God to Bethlehem — and to Calvary.

Santa on a Cross?

In an essay I read a while back, the writer described an American visitor to Japan who was walking through a Tokyo department store during the Christmas season. It was obvious the Japanese had begun to make considerable use of the Christmas symbols that are all-too-familiar to Westerners. But the visitor was not prepared for one combination of images he encountered: Santa Claus nailed to a cross.

I have heard enough sermons condemning the commercialization of Christmas to know what most Christians would make of this composite image. Here we have in a stark display, they would tell us, a symbol of all that is bad about our Christmas celebrations. Not only have we taken the Christ out of Christmas, we have even taken him down from the Cross — to be replaced by a symbol of the worst of Yuletide greed.

Behold, Santa Claus, the new consumerist savior!

Still, maybe we can see the picture in another way.

To be sure, the commercialization of Christmas is an obvious fact of contemporary life. But there is often a breakthrough in the Christmas season of something very different: We might call it the "Christmas-ization of commerce." In the midst of all the consumerist hoopla come genuine outbreaks of goodwill and a sacrificial spirit. And when this happens, Santa Claus can serve a large and noble purpose.

Actually, the perspective of the Tokyo merchandiser who put Santa on a cross isn't so far removed from that of our own children. In her book *Flights of Fancy, Leaps of Faith,* Cindy Dell Clark reports on interviews she conducted with children about their favorite holiday legends. She discovered a strong desire to integrate the Santa story with the Christian narrative. Not only did the children think of Santa as a guide to moral development ("He knows if you've been naughty, he knows if you've been nice"), they also linked him directly to the God of the Bible. One six-year-old boy asserted confidently that God and Santa are next-door neighbors. A girl of the same age reported that Santa distributes his gifts on direct orders from the Lord.

I think these children are onto something. Santa Claus certainly has a prominent marketing role in the Christmas season, but that is not his whole job description. To see Santa as a mere consumer icon is also to have a reductionist view of human nature.

We humans are not mere consumers. We are

driven by deeper impulses than those that are shaped by market forces. "Thou hast made us for Thyself, and our hearts are restless until they rest in Thee," says St. Augustine in the opening paragraph of his *Confessions*. During the Christmas season our need for such things as belonging, forgiveness, and security can surface in dramatic ways. And none of our often frantic attempts to surround ourselves with sights and sounds and tastes of a consumerist culture can really speak to the longings that arise from the deep places in our souls.

Long ago, Santa Claus began his career as a fourth-century Christian bishop who was named a saint after his death. Saint Nicholas was known for his love of gift-giving, especially to children. The story goes that in the dark of night he would leave gifts at the houses of those in need. He came to be admired as a servant of a Gospel that teaches us that even though we have rebelled against God, He has graciously offered a salvation that we could never find by our own efforts. As time went on, the legends expanded, and Saint Nicholas evolved into our present-day Santa Claus. And while Santa Claus does get co-opted for many purposes these days, he has never completely abandoned his commitment to moral accountability and unselfish giving.

Unlike much of the other mythology that has built up around the Christmas celebration, the original Christmas story, telling about a heaven-sent Savior who was born at Bethlehem, has the marvelous feature of being true. There really is, as the angel told the shepherds, "good news of great joy for all the people."

Santa Claus did not die for our sins. In important ways, though, the man in the red suit still does minister on the side of the angels. So it is not so far-fetched to think that Santa can at least point us to that wonderful gift that was made possible by the One who did go from the manger to the Cross.

The Jesus Factor

I once had a science teacher who had created what he considered to be a no-nonsense method for assigning grades in his courses. Your final letter grade was based on how many points you had accumulated throughout the semester. The points, in turn, could be earned in a variety of ways: daily quizzes, lab reports, a lengthy mid-term test, and a final exam. If, by the time the final exam came along, you had already built up enough points for a "B" or a "C," and if you were content with that grade, you could skip the final. Or you could take it easy for a while earlier on, skipping quizzes and lab reports, and hope that by cramming you could get the points you needed on one of the big tests.

The teacher — who also let it be known that he had no use for religious beliefs — had a clever way of introducing his points-system to his classes. "There is no Jesus Factor in this course," he would announce.

I have often wished that I had asked him what he

meant exactly by a "Jesus Factor." But I think I have some idea. He wanted to eliminate all subjective factors from his grading. In his classroom, you got what you earned, and what it took to earn enough points was clearly spelled out. If the dog ate your homework, or your grandmother died, or there was a power outage and your alarm clock did not wake you up — tough! No excuses: "show me the points!" In a word, there was no room for *mercy* in his system, and he was proud of it.

Actually, his system worked quite well. He may have been a bit too rigid in his attitudes, but his total-points method was quite appropriate for a biology course.

But I'm glad that when it comes to dealing with the larger issues of life, there is indeed a Jesus Factor. Mercy is what the Gospel is really all about. If the Lord were simply to add up the points earned, we would all be miserable failures. But the marvelous thing is that "He hath not dealt with us after our sins; nor rewarded us according to our iniquities" (Psalm 103:10). God sent us a Savior. On the Cross, Jesus did what we could not accomplish on our own behalf. This is the real Jesus Factor.

The nineteenth-century preacher Charles Spurgeon put it well: "The doctrine of the atonement is to my mind one of the surest proofs of the divine inspiration of Holy Scripture. Who would or could have thought of the just Ruler dying for the unjust rebel? This is no teaching of human mythology, or dream of poetical imagination. This method of expiation is only known among men because it is a fact; fiction could not have devised it. God Himself ordained it; it is not a matter which could have been imagined."

As a teacher, I operate with high expectations. Like my science professor, I also generally use a "show-me-the-points" approach in evaluating my students' work. But I am glad that when we all face the *real* final test — the Last Judgment — God isn't going to pass me or fail me on the basis of my ability to show the points. On that Day, the Jesus Factor will be my only hope.

Sin versus Ignorance

I was in a bad mood the morning I drove to a nearby college campus to serve on an interreligious panel. I had agreed to the assignment many months before, but when the day came I resented having to give up a Saturday for the event.

But when it was all over I was glad I had done it. The topic was peacemaking, and my fellow panelists were a rabbi, a local Muslim leader, a Hindu, and a Buddhist. Each of us was asked to give a ten-minute presentation on how our religious community views the basic moral issues relating to war and peace. Then we would pose questions to each other, and after that we would interact with the audience.

I was the leadoff speaker. I quoted those wonderful passages from the Old Testament where the prophets envision a day when swords will be beaten into plowshares and all warfare will be banished from the earth. I also explained some of Jesus' teachings on the subject. Christians, I said, must be committed to peacemaking. But we also know that sinfulness typically rules the day in our present world. We fallen creatures are inclined to follow our own rebellious impulses. Until God ushers in the new creation at the return of Christ, we cannot expect a lasting peace. But that is no reason for us simply to give our lives over to violent solutions. As followers of Christ, we must do all that we can to protect innocent people from the ravages of warfare, even as we also witness to a better way, the way of pursuing God's *shalom*.

The rabbi came next, and he began by announcing that "the Christian guy also gave the Jewish perspective." Except for my references to Jesus as the Christ, he said, he could endorse all that I said. He spent the rest of his time elaborating on some of the themes that I had introduced.

Much to my surprise, the Muslim led off by saying that he agreed with the basic ideas that the rabbi and I had set forth. He quoted and explained many passages from the Qur'an whose contents paralleled the teachings of the Bible.

The spirit of unity was broken, though, by the Hindu. The three previous panelists, he observed, all seemed to believe in original sin. "This is not the Hindu understanding of why things go wrong in the world," he argued. "We believe — not in *original sin* — but in *original ignorance*. The basic solution is not to be saved from sin — rather, we need to be enlightened."

His basic perspective was immediately endorsed by the Buddhist panelist. We do not need to be rescued by some power outside of ourselves, she said. We must cultivate the knowledge that exists within each of our spirits.

And so the lines were drawn. Sin versus ignorance. Salvation versus enlightenment. I'm sure that if we were given more time, the Jew and the Muslim and I would have found some important things to disagree about. (For example, Jews and Muslims typically do not like the Christian phrase "original sin.") But in this context we sounded similar themes. Left to our own, we human beings are in big trouble. We desperately need help "from above." And we are naturally inclined to resist that help. Our rebellious wills must be tamed, and we must find the way of obedience to the will of our Creator. More knowledge alone will not rescue us from our human predicament.

I have thought often about that discussion since the events of September 11, 2001. Tensions among Christians, Jews, and Muslims have never been stronger. Shouldn't we, as representatives of the three communities, be engaging in detailed discussions together about how we understand the fundamental realities of sin and salvation? Aren't our respective views about such matters as religious teachers more important than the advice we might want to offer our governments about military policy and international affairs?

The fundamental questions that are at stake here

are always urgent ones: What is the basic problem? And what is the basic solution?

Here is the answer I accept with all my heart: Christ Jesus came into the world to save sinners. What a wonderful message that is to proclaim to a broken and confused humanity — and to talk about with friends from other religious groups.

What about Hell?

"I have this theological problem I need to talk about. It's about hell." The student sitting in my office was a thoughtful and enthusiastic Christian. If Susan had a theological problem, I knew it was something I had to take seriously. "I just can't understand how a good God can send people to hell for all eternity." Now her voice began to tremble: "I feel guilty even thinking these thoughts, because I know what the Bible teaches. I just have such a hard time fitting hell into my own experience of God's love!"

I told Susan she did not need to feel guilty. Her question was a good one and she was asking it in just the right way. I told her about some advice I once received from a wise Christian leader: "There are two kinds of people who have problems with the idea of hell," he had said. "One group thinks that we're too good to be punished by God. The other group thinks that God is too good to punish us. The second group is asking the healthy question."

Susan was clearly in the second group. As we continued to talk, it became clear that she wanted unbelievers to "taste and see that the LORD is good" (Psalm 34:8). She knew that the mercy that can be found at the Cross of Jesus is greater than all our sin.

Some Christians give the impression that they take delight in the idea of hell. But the Bible makes it clear that the Lord "is not wanting any to perish, but all to come to repentence" (2 Peter 3:9). As Susan and I discussed, I emphasized human freedom. God does not want people to suffer the agonies of hell. If people go there, it is by their own choice. As C. S. Lewis put it, the door to hell is locked from the inside. Hell isn't what God does to people; it is what people do to themselves.

Susan came back with a good question. Doesn't the Bible itself talk about hell as something that God *does* to us? Unrepentant sinners "will be *thrown* into the outer darkness, where there will be weeping and gnashing of teeth" (Matthew 8:12), and the wicked will be "*thrown* into the lake of fire" (Revelation 20:15). This is indeed the way the Bible sometimes puts it. But we need to remind ourselves that this is biblical *imagery*. We can't take the "throwing" imagery literally, any more than we should insist on a literal outer darkness and a literal lake of fire. These images are graphic reminders that it is a terrible thing to cut ourselves off from the love of God.

Susan pressed with more questions. What about God's power? If God can do anything, can't he fix it so that people will not persist in rejecting him? This is precisely where we must stay focused on God's love, I responded. When we humans love someone with a healthy love, we know that we cannot manipulate them into making the right responses. Even when it breaks our hearts, we refuse to force ourselves on those we love. God is the greatest Lover in the universe. Jesus showed us the grieving heart of God when he wept over the rebellious inhabitants of Jerusalem.

At the end of our conversation, Susan was not done with her questioning. Neither am I. Someday God will make it plainer for us. But she and I agreed: it is enough for now to rest in God's goodness, inviting others to join us in knowing the embrace of a loving Savior.

Oversize Religion

B rowsing in a large bookstore recently, I made my way to the religion section. The shelves carried the usual signs: "Eastern Religions," "Judaism," "Occult," "Christianity." But a bottom shelf filled with tall books carried a label I had not seen before: "Oversize Religion."

I like the idea of a religion that is oversize. It reminds us of the need to resist the tendency in our culture to keep religion in its "place": our personal faith is a private matter, we are told. It's OK to talk about God in church, but we shouldn't go parading our beliefs in public!

This will not do. The God of the Bible cannot be confined to limited spaces. "Who can hide in secret places so that I cannot see them? says the LORD. Do I not fill heaven and earth?" (Jeremiah 23:24). We need an oversize God, because we human beings have an oversize problem — our sinfulness. The problem is far too big to settle on our own. Only a God of infinite mercy can save us.

A number of spiritual writers talk about the fact that we human beings are created with a "God-sized hunger," a profound yearning in our souls that nothing less than God can satisfy. This hunger can express itself in various ways: an oversize guilt; an oversize loneliness; an oversize desire to know "what it is all about"; an oversize fear of the future; an oversize passion for justice. Only an oversize God can satisfy these longings in the deep places of our lives.

A reporter called me once to ask how evangelical Christians might react if intelligent life were to be discovered on some other planet. I asked her whether she had ever attended a Billy Graham evangelistic meeting, and she told me that she had once been sent to cover one. Did they sing, "How Great Thou Art" that night? I asked. She could not remember. So I quoted some lines for her: "O Lord, my God/When I in awesome wonder/Consider all the worlds thy hand hath made. . . . Then sings my soul, my Savior God, to thee:/ How great thou art!" If I am around when they discover life on other planets, I told her, I would just start singing that hymn: ". . . all the worlds thy hand hath made."

That is what the Gospel is all about — an oversize God who creates an oversize universe and an oversize God who saves us through his oversize love and grace.

The Center of the Universe

My wife and I regularly attend the National Prayer Breakfast. It is always an exciting event. But for me the first time brought the biggest thrill. We were sitting at a table near the front of the large banquet hall and we had a great view of the distinguished lineup at the head table on the platform: the Bushes, the Quayles, Colin Powell, distinguished members of Congress, and others.

I was seated next to a young Muslim, a diplomat from one of the Middle Eastern embassies. In our brief conversation I asked him how long he had been in Washington. Less than a year, was the answer. I asked him what it was like for him to live and work in our nation's capital. He smiled. "We're not supposed to say this kind of thing," he said, "but this is a wonderful place to be." And then he added a comment, gesturing toward the platform as he made it: "Washington is the center of the universe!"

There wasn't any time to continue the conversation, so I did not have a chance to tell him about my map of the universe. It is described in Colossians 1: "In him" — in Jesus Christ — "all things in heaven and on earth were created, things visible and invisible . . . and in him all things hold together."

We don't have to be in Washington or any other gathering of the humanly powerful to experience being at the center of the universe. We are there whenever we are in the presence of Jesus Christ. And, of course, Christians know that we are *always* in his presence. Sometimes that is a disturbing thought. When I am in one of my especially rebellious moods, I am often caught up short by the awareness that my thoughts and deeds are completely transparent to Christ.

But living with an awareness that we are at the center of the universe at all times can also be a marvelous comfort. Not long before Jesus left his disciples to return to heaven, he told them to "remember, I am with you always, to the end of the age" (Matthew 28:20). That is the comforting part. There is nothing we can experience — no hardship, temptation, fear, depression, illness — that does not take place in the presence of our Savior. We are always at the center of the universe — even "to the end of the age."

CHURCH AND WORLD

Sister Helen's Tears

S ome of my Catholic friends were reminiscing recently about the Irish nuns who taught them in parochial schools. As an evangelical Calvinist who to this day has never set foot inside a Catholic grammar school, I kept a respectful silence while they talked. But I came close to knowing what they were talking about. Miss O'Connell, my seventh-grade public school teacher wasn't a nun at the time. But she entered a convent at the end of our year together. I even have a sneaking suspicion that I gave her a little nudge in that direction.

Most of the women who taught me during my four years in the Watervliet, New York, public school system were Irish Catholics: Miss O'Brien, Miss Byrne, and Miss Fogarty dominated my world in those days.

And the nun-to-be, Helen O'Connell. She was both very Irish and very Catholic. If anyone had ever mentioned the separation of church and state to Miss O'Connell, I'm sure she would have thought the idea preposterous. To be sure, the Lord's Prayer, the Ten Commandments, and "God Bless America" were the standard fare of everyday public school piety in the early 1950s. But Miss O'Connell was not one to settle for generic civil religion. She made the sign of the cross at our opening devotions, and her classroom conversation was liberally sprinkled with references to the Holy Father and the Blessed Virgin and — one of her favorite subjects — the Blarney Stone.

I flustered Miss O'Connell. Mainly, she was irritated with the smart-aleck and know-it-all I so often was in those days. But Miss O'Connell's frustration also had to do more specifically with my tendency to issue theological challenges to her reflexive Catholicism. "We Protestants don't believe in the Pope," I would tell her in the middle of one of her brief classroom homilies. Then her neck would begin to redden, followed by a full-scale blush and then a nervous transition into another topic.

She made her announcement on the last day of regular classes in our seventh grade school year. "I have something to tell you, boys and girls" — the blush was already there and we knew it was an important topic. "I am leaving this school. God has called me to be a nun. I will soon be entering the convent." She quickly turned to record some final piece of classroom business on the blackboard. But just before she did — just as she finished saying the word "convent" — she glanced in my direction. Our eyes met for only an instant. Hers were full of tears. Much to my surprise, I too felt like crying. Hours later, alone in my bedroom, I did let the tears flow.

I have wondered many times since whether Miss O'Connell's tears that day had anything specifically to do with me. Was she worried about my soul? Had she come to think of me as one of her spiritual-pedagogical failures? Did our little religious tug-of-war have anything to do with her decision to take the habit? Could it even be that she felt, in the spiritual passion of my own classroom argumentativeness, a kindred spirit?

In my more rational moments I think I must be exaggerating the significance of that tearful glance. Surely my worries have more to do with my own memories of adolescent awkwardness than with the inner workings of Helen O'Connell's soul. But for all of that, the questions have nagged me over the decades. And so one night a year or so ago, when I was back near Watervliet on business, I began dialing from my motel room the numbers of the O'Connells listed in the phone book, asking about a Helen O'Connell who had been my seventh-grade teacher in a public school just before she had become a nun.

On the fourth attempt I connected. "I'm sure you're talking about a distant cousin of my husband's," the woman said. "I never really got to know Sister Helen," she said. "But I did meet her once at a family gathering. Unfortunately, though, you're a little too late to contact her. I read in the paper a month or so ago that she died."

I had wanted to write Sister Helen a letter. I wanted to tell her that I am sorry for my youthful arrogance. I wanted to tell her that I co-chair the Los Angeles Evangelical-Roman Catholic Dialogue, that I enjoy reading Henri Nouwen, and that sometimes I go to a Benedictine monastery to pray. I also wanted to tell her that even though I lacked the categories for saying so on that last day of seventh grade, I admired her decision to become a nun, that even then I knew deep in my heart that she was doing this because she loved God so very much.

It was too late to write that letter to Sister Helen. But recently I found myself once again near Watervliet. After preaching at a church service in a nearby city on a Sunday morning, I drove to what had been Miss O'Connell's parish church. The late morning mass at St. Patrick's was still going on when I got there. I knelt with the rest of the worshipers for the prayers of the people.

When the congregation prayed for the souls of those who have died, I thanked the Lord for Helen O'Connell and for the mystery of those tears that she shed on the day she told us that she had been called to be a nun. I thanked God for Vatican II, and for all of the good things that have been happening in Protestant-Catholic relationships since the last day of my seventh-grade school year. And I asked the Lord to forgive the spiritual arrogance, not only of a thirteen-year-old school boy, but of an adult evangelical who has not yet lost all of the spiritual smart-alecky-ness that lurked in that adolescent soul. And kneeling there in Helen O'Connell's church, I once again shed a few tears.

A Prayer to Mary

Recently I read another evangelical critique of Roman Catholicism's devotion to Mary. I was in basic agreement with the points that it made. I find it difficult to know why Roman Catholics say what they do about the status of Mary.

Still, I wish that the tone of the criticisms had been a little gentler. While my theological convictions on this topic are still firm, my mood has gotten a little softer ever since the afternoon I found myself breathing a short but heart-felt prayer to the Holy Mother.

It was in a cathedral in northern France, on a lazy summer day in July of 1987. As a way to give some focus to our vacation wanderings, my wife and I were making a special point of visiting Gothic cathedrals.

As we approached this particular cathedral, a young couple on a motorcycle pulled up. They were in their late teens, and they were very punk. Both were dressed in black. His hair was spiked, hers dyed orange. Her face was heavily painted in white and black.

I was curious about why they were visiting a cathedral. So while my wife studied the art, I followed this couple at a discreet distance as they walked around.

Actually, they swaggered. I caught nothing of their conversation, but their insolence was unmistakable. She would point at something derisively, and he would snort. Then he would point and she would snort. Whatever the purpose of their visit, I decided, it had nothing to do with either a spiritual or an aesthetic appreciation for Gothic cathedrals.

I lingered longer than they did at the high altar, so I don't know how the change of mood occurred. But when I came upon them again, she was standing near a statue of the Virgin Mary in a side chapel, while he was a little ways off, looking at a painting. The young woman was staring directly into the Holy Mother's face. Mary's eyes were directed toward a little kneeling bench at her feet, and her hands were outstretched.

Suddenly the young woman lurched toward the bench and knelt before the Virgin. Face buried in her arms, she began to sob. Her companion turned and saw her. His face registered shock.

I moved on. Many minutes later, I made my way back to the side chapel. The young woman was just standing up from the kneeling bench. She looked into the Virgin's face, then turned to her friend. Her punk makeup was almost all washed away, and her eyes were very red. She held out her hand, and he took it. Slowly, and without a word, they walked away.

I don't really understand what happened to that young woman that afternoon, and I probably never will. But I'm glad that she knelt before the Virgin. My hunch is that it was very good for her to shed those tears.

I hope so. I think about that young woman often. And when I remember her, I pray to God on her behalf.

On that afternoon, though, I prayed to the Holy Mother. After the couple left, I sat in a pew in the side chapel and looked into the face of the statue. "Mary," I asked, "please don't let her wander far. Keep her safe, and lead her to your Son."

That is the only time I have ever addressed a petition to the Virgin Mary. I don't know whether that one prayer makes me guilty of "Mariolatry" or not. Nor has that question troubled me much.

The theology that I instinctively operated with on that summer afternoon may have been confused. But I still sense that my prayer arrived at the right destination.

Only One Evangel

On two different occasions in my life I heard the evangel — the Gospel story — in a way that profoundly reoriented my way of viewing things.

The first occurred in 1957 at a Billy Graham evangelistic service in New York's Madison Square Garden. I was a teenager, and I had frequently been traveling to the nightly "crusade" meeting with our New Jersey church group. But on this night several of my high school friends, none of them churchgoers, had come along out of curiosity. That evening Mr. Graham spoke directly to teenagers — calling on us to "take a stand for Jesus Christ." I had always considered myself to be a Christian, but in those moments I felt an urge coming from some deep place in my spirit to make a very personal and public commitment — in front of my teenage friends — to the Savior that the evangelist was proclaiming. As the mass choir sang "Just as I am, without one plea," I walked down the aisle to ask the

Lord Jesus to come into my life in a very personal way. I still look back on that evening as a major milestone in my spiritual life.

The second event was much less public. In 1963, just a few days before I registered for my first courses as a philosophy graduate student, I sat in a living room watching the live broadcast of Martin Luther King's "I Have a Dream" speech. I had been sympathetic to the civil rights movement all along, but on this occasion — hearing Dr. King's profoundly moving call to justice — I felt that same urge in the deep places that I had experienced at the Billy Graham service. The tears flowed, and I quietly prayed that I would always be faithful to the prophetic call that I heard that day. This too was a major milestone.

With all the publicity being given these days to "the Christian Right," it takes some effort to remember that there was a time, as recent as twenty-five years ago, when evangelical Christians were regularly criticized for being a-political. But that was how it was when I had my second "conversion" while watching the March on Washington. We white folks who liked Billy Graham weren't supposed to get enthusiastic about Martin Luther King as well. The "Social Gospel" was the sort of thing that liberal Protestants preached. We knew that the real message was an evangel about "personal salvation."

But I could not set aside the deep conviction that my two experiences were intimately connected — that the same Spirit who called out to me at the Billy Graham meeting was summoning me now to support the cause of racial justice. Each of my experiences, I was convinced, had to do with the same evangel. In both instances I was responding to the same message of good news. The evangel was surely a word about personal forgiveness. Jesus died for me, and by accepting that fact in a very individual way I could experience the benefit that the choir was singing about as I walked down the aisle: "Just as I am, thou wilt receive, wilt welcome, pardon, cleanse, relieve, because thy promise I believe. . . ." But the message also included a more far-reaching word of good news. The Jesus who died to save individuals was also a Lord who wanted to make the crooked places plain and justice to roll down like a mighty river. His heart was grieved by prejudice and oppression. He hated racism, and he wanted human beings to live together in peace and harmony.

Properly understood — or so I firmly believe — the two aspects of the evangel, personal salvation and social justice, presuppose each other. To be fully "saved" is to be incorporated into a community of disciples who do their Lord's bidding — a Lord who cares deeply about the corporate dimensions of our human existence. No one understood this better than the African American slave community. They knew that in the midst of life's worst trials, they could as individuals "steal away to Jesus." But they also knew that this Jesus was the revelation of the same God who constantly demands that the oppressive rulers of this world "let my people go."

But a commitment to justice, if it is to be carried out for the long haul, needs also to draw on the sustaining resources of a very personal faith. Dr. King's message itself gave evidence of this: he proclaimed the message of structural righteousness with the testimony that "*I* have a dream." The same blending of the "we" and the "I" occurs in the great civil rights hymn: "Deep in *my* heart *I* do believe, *we* shall overcome someday."

The Christian evangel integrates these two emphases in a marvelous way. The Jesus who saves individuals is also the Lord of creation. Through his death and resurrection he has decisively overcome sin and death, sealing the doom of all that stands against God's creating and redeeming purposes in the world. There are not two evangels, one for individual souls and another for the world at large. To know Jesus the Savior properly is to understand, in the words of the wonderful advent song, that "he comes to make his blessings flow, far as the curse is found, far as the curse is found."

Confessions of an "Oppressor"

I was the guest preacher at a large congregation in a city in Texas and, after the third and final service of the morning, was greeting people at the door. One man had been standing off by himself, and when all the others had finally left, he approached me to talk. With the cut of his beard and his mode of dress, he resembled an Amish farmer. He was carrying a tall plain wooden walking stick. When I offered my hand, he refused to shake it.

"Sir," he began, "one of the psalms you talked about this morning says that the Lord 'executes justice for the oppressed.' Do you know that *you* are one of the oppressors?" I wasn't expecting this, but I did manage to stammer something about being aware that I am a sinner in need of God's mercy. "No, sir! You are not just a sinner. You are an *oppressor*." I asked him what kind of oppression he had in mind. "By training all of these people in your school to become corrupt shepherds, you are oppressing us all. You don't want to hear that — but it is a word from the Lord!" He turned and walked away.

On any other day I might have simply chuckled to myself, passing this off as another oddball who had a thing about the organized church. But earlier that morning, in my hotel room, I had read the latest newspaper accounts of clergy scandals. The focus this time around was on Roman Catholic priests, but only a few days before I had been told about yet another evangelical leader who had been involved in a sordid affair. On this particular day, the self-styled prophet who delivered his stern message to me was hitting pretty close to home!

For those who want to be cynical about church leadership these days, there is plenty of evidence to work with. But there is also evidence that can give us hope. Just the day before my conversation with my accuser, I had spent several hours in another Texas city at one of the events we put on in places where there are significant numbers of Fuller graduates, friends of the seminary, and prospective students. I had a chance to listen to some of my colleagues talk about their present teaching and research interests, and I was inspired by what I heard. We have a magnificent faculty — people who are deeply committed to promoting the cause of Christ's Kingdom.

But I was also impressed with the representatives of two generations of Fuller folks who visited with us that day — those who have graduated from our seminary and those who are planning to join us in the near future. In both groups there was much passion: our alums were passionate about using what they were taught at Fuller to have an impact on the church and the world; our future students were passionate about the Gospel and eager to learn all that they can to follow the Lord's call in their lives.

This is not a time for cynicism about Christian leadership. To be sure, we must take an honest look at the failures that keep producing scandals. My awkward response to the Texas prophet was an appropriate one: we leaders are sinners who are completely dependent upon God's mercy. And the wonderful thing is that the Lord is indeed "merciful and gracious, slow to anger and abounding in steadfast love" (Psalm 103:8). At the same time, this merciful God holds us accountable for the way in which we exercise our leadership.

Mercy and accountability — two crucial themes these days for all of us who are committed to promoting the cause of the Gospel.

Patriotism

In the weeks following the horrors of 9/11, I had a streak of patriotic feelings. It was good to see people flying flags and wearing flag-pins on their clothes. And for a spell it felt good to get choked up during the singing of the National Anthem. But after a while, the feelings toned down a bit.

Note that I am talking about feelings here. I have always had a basic loyalty to my country. I have never had much patience with cynical America-bashing. But I have not typically been able to get very emotional about the issues of citizenship. Much of this is because I am very much a product of the 1960s. I had serious doubts about the war in Vietnam in my youth, and this was not a popular stance to take in the evangelical world in those days. Evangelical Christians were often super-patriotic. "My country, right or wrong!" was one of their rallying cries.

I had real theological problems with that attitude.

That kind of patriotism struck me as bordering on idolatry. The worship — or near-worship — of a nation is a serious problem from a biblical perspective. We live in a fallen world, and governments and governmental leaders are not exempted from the patterns of our sinfulness. This is why democracy is such a healthy way of structuring our collective lives. It allows for continuing debate about our policies — even for legitimate protest.

According to the New Testament, governments are an important part of the divine plan, "for there is no authority except from God, and those authorities that exist have been instituted by God" (Romans 13:1). But the apostle who says this also makes it clear that this does not give a government license to do whatever it wants: political leaders should not be "a terror to good conduct, but to bad" (Romans 13:3). If a government encourages bad policies and practices, it is misusing its God-given authority. So we must never offer our uncritical obedience to a human government. Absolute loyalty is something that only God deserves from us.

That's the kind of thing I started to worry much about in the 1960s. And, frankly, it made it difficult for me ever since to allow my patriotic feelings to flow freely. So it was a good experience for me recently to experience those emotions.

There is nothing wrong with patriotism as such. Indeed it can be a very healthy thing. The Bible often uses the word "honor" in describing what Christians should cultivate in their dealings with the nations in which they live. That's the same word that is applied in the Ten Commandments to our parental relations: "Honor your father and your mother" (Exodus 20:12). The link between parents and nation is a good one to think about. There is a natural connection. "Patriotism" comes from the word for "father." We often speak of our "fatherland" or our "motherland."

There is nothing wrong with feeling sentimental about our parents. It can even be a nice thing on occasion to get carried away with those emotions. When a mother gets a card from a son that says "You are the Greatest Mom in the World," she has every right simply to enjoy the compliment. Strictly speaking, of course, what the son is saying is a gross exaggeration. Not every woman who gets a Mother's Day greeting with that sentiment can possibly be the Greatest Mom in the World. But the hyperbole is OK. We all understand what is going on. And we all know that any woman who took the claim literally could be dangerous!

For similar reasons, there is nothing inappropriate as such in thinking of my own country as the Greatest Nation in the World. Sentimental hyperbole is one of the ways we express important affections. But there is a special danger when we say such things about our country. Nations have a tendency to believe that they really *are* the greatest. And nations, especially powerful nations like the United States, have a lot of guns and bombs in their possession. When they start backing up their belief in their own greatness by using these bombs and guns against other nations, they can become serious threats.

I am no pacifist. I support campaigns against international terrorism and favor using our military for restoring justice. But I reserve the right also to criticize my government if I think they are misusing their power. And I will always be on guard against expressing my affection for my country in a way that encourages our leaders to take our expressions of affection too literally. I take this view because I believe strongly in democracy. But even more important, I take it because I worry about the ever-present threat of idolatry.

Nursing Fathers

The political leader must be a "nursing father." That was a surprising image I ran across a few years ago, when I was studying the political views of seventeenth-century Scottish Presbyterian theologians.

What caught me off guard was not only the striking imagery, but also the context in which it appeared. These Calvinist writers were not especially fond of gentle formulations. They certainly did not seem otherwise given to the language of nurture. They were pretty stern folks who did not go out of their way to use words that evoked pictures of intimate relationships. And yet in this one instance they employed the language of tenderness in describing the duties of political leadership.

Presidential inauguration ceremonies in the United States are also good opportunities for a change of tone. Even if the shift in mood is only temporary, it is healthy to declare a "time out" in order to remind ourselves of the larger purposes that we serve as a nation. In our election campaigns we devote much energy to the give-and-take of partisan politics. This is the stuff— for all of its obvious excesses — on which a democracy thrives. But it is also necessary now and then to step back and look at the bigger picture, to reflect together on the ways in which our patterns of governance can promote our common good.

The period of Scottish history I was studying was a time of much turmoil. My Calvinist writers were involved in major disputes with Roman Catholics and Anglicans — and even with other Presbyterians! — and the arguments often took the form of quite violent struggles for political power. Any form of political compromise was, as one of the Presbyterians put it, "an abomination." In his scheme of things, toleration was . . . well, it was intolerable.

These people liked the Old Testament, and they drew heavily from its pages in expressing their political views. Their God was a divine Ruler who wanted his chosen people, his "new Israel," to conform to standards not unlike those that he required of the ancient Israelites. If the Scottish nation did not live up to those standards, then the country was in deep trouble. Thus the revealing title of one of the works I read: *The Causes of God's Wrath Against Scotland.*

But then, in the midst of all of this harsh rhetoric, there were these occasional references to breast-feeding in political life. One writer, for example, criticized a particular king because he failed to be a "nursing father." And another insisted that God requires kings to serve their nations as "fathers, nurses, protectors, [and] guides."

Here, too, these Presbyterian divines were showing that they took their Old Testament loyalties very seriously. They were drawing on some obscure imagery used on only a few occasions in the King James Version of the Old Testament. The breast-feeding image is applied to royalty twice in the book of Isaiah, and these Calvinist writers undoubtedly had these references in mind: "And kings shall be thy nursing fathers, and their queens thy nursing mothers" (49:23); "Thou . . . shalt suck the breast of kings" (60:16).

This is not the kind of imagery that most preachers these days would choose to feature in their sermon titles. But it is not a bad idea to keep it in mind when we witness the very public ceremonies of leadership transition in the United States. On this one point at least, we can learn something from the political instincts of these old Presbyterian writers. Here is the basic point: *God wants political leaders to be nurturers.*

Psalm 72 uses a slightly different nurturing image. The description here is of a righteous king: "He shall come down like rain upon the mown grass: as showers that water the earth" (v. 6). This is said in a context where the psalm writer is celebrating the reign of a king who cares about the poor and wants to "save the children of the needy" (v. 4).

The United States is not a monarchy. To draw the proper parallel from the Old Testament texts to our own context is to think of our three branches of national government — the president and his cabinet, the Congress, the courts — collectively as the "king" who is obligated to "feed" the nation. This is not about food handouts, of course — although they may be required in some circumstances. The feeding here is by a nurturing spirit that cares about the well-being of all of the people, with special attention to "the needy." Governments are obliged by God to foster a climate of peace and righteousness for all the people.

Obviously, there is much to debate here about what this means for practical policy. Those are good debates to have. I have changed my mind on policy matters many times in my adult life — and I continue to argue these matters, not only with other people, but even in my own mind and heart. The issues of public peace and righteousness are complex ones. And, unlike many of my Calvinist ancestors, I know that I have to cultivate a healthy spirit of tolerance in the pluralistic society in which I live.

But I do want governments to nurture, to promote a caring spirit, and to call all of us to recognize the need to work for a common good. The ceremonies of national transition are good occasions for reminding ourselves of this need. In a democracy, we are all part of the government. Our national ceremonies remind us of our fundamental obligations as citizens. As we inaugurate a new leadership team, the nursing-parent image is a good one for "we, the people," to keep in mind.

Our "Post" World

"Post-Christian." "Post-modern." "Post-Enlightenment." There is a lot of "posting" going on these days. These three labels are expressions of a similar mood. Many people today have a profound sense of living in a time of "afters." After Christianity, after modernity, after the Enlightenment.

Needless to say, if our world really is "post-Christian" in the sense that Christian faith and witness is merely a thing of the past, then churches and seminaries might as well shut down. We know that we have not moved beyond the need for the Gospel. But if to be post-Christian means to be "after Christendom," then the label is quite accurate. Christian institutions are no longer a dominant factor in shaping our lives as citizens, neighbors, and participants in the marketplace. Whether Christians should have ever thought that they should try to extend their influence through institutionalized power is a good question for theological debate. Not every Christian would answer the question in quite the same way. But the arguments seem rather abstract these days. "Christendom" is surely a thing of the past.

The widespread disillusionment today, however, goes well beyond recognizing a rejection of the church's corporate influence. The "post-modern" and "post-Enlightenment" moods signal a rejection of some important secular philosophies as well. A century ago many intellectuals were excited about living in "modern" times. They were very optimistic about what the "enlightened" human consciousness could achieve in the world. People believed in *progress*. They were convinced that the world was getting better, and that many of the problems that had long plagued the human race — war, poverty, superstition, prejudice — would soon give way to the advance of science, technology, and other ventures of the human spirit.

That dream of progress has turned into a nightmare. Instead of an enlightened culture, we seem to be slipping into more darkness. And it is increasingly difficult for many of our contemporaries to believe that there is a light at the end of the tunnel.

I am not pessimistic, though. Do we live in difficult times? Of course. Do the problems seem insoluble? They certainly do. But God's "heavenly sunshine" has not been extinguished. We may be living in a post-Christendom age, but these are not "post-Christ" times! "All things came into being through him, and without him not one thing came into being. What has come into being in him was life, and the life was the light of all people. The light shines in the darkness, and the darkness did not overcome it" (John 1:3-5).

Eating Alone

Civil society is in big trouble. At least that is what a number of social commentators having been telling us lately. By "civil society" they mean that broad network of associations and relationships in free societies that stand between the individual and the state: clubs, teams, neighborhood groups, churches, PTAs, veterans organizations, fraternities, sororities, and service clubs. Without these things we run the risk of either getting caught up in a fragmenting individualism on the one hand or being absorbed into a totalitarian political system on the other. They help to give us our sense of social identity. And the evidence seems to show that these ways of relating to each other are in serious decline.

Robert Putnam is one scholar who worries much about this pattern. He is a Harvard professor who has studied the role of voluntary associations in promoting a healthy society. These days, argues Putnam, we are living off inherited "social capital," a fund from the past of community values and social reinforcements that is now in danger of being depleted. In his much discussed book, *Bowling Alone,* Professor Putnam offers evidence that people simply are not getting together in the ways that once flourished. His provocative title comes from one of his key examples. Membership in bowling leagues has been in a serious decline in recent years. At the same time, though, more people are bowling than ever before. The result is the "bowling alone" syndrome.

Not everyone agrees with Putnam's general point. Some are convinced that he hasn't done justice to some new ways in which people are forming social bonds. Maybe, for example, the reason why young marrieds don't join bowling leagues these days is that they are too busy attending their kids' soccer games. Or maybe they are too involved in the activities sponsored by the new mega-churches. Or maybe they are spending too much time in on-line chat rooms.

Those are good things to argue about. But I hope that in these debates we don't miss one specific point that Putnam makes, almost in passing. The decline in bowling leagues, he observes, has caused some real problems for bowling alleys. When people bowl in teams they tend to sit around and eat together. Bowling establishments count on the sale of hot dogs, pizza, and beer for many of their profits. And people who don't socialize when they bowl also don't buy much food at bowling alleys. Bowling alone means eating alone.

However else we might want to evaluate the current debates about civil society, I am convinced of this much: eating alone is a big social problem. We ought to be especially worried about the virtual disappearance of the daily family meal. The companies that operate college cafeterias tell us that students today don't dine — they "graze." They seldom relax for a whole meal eaten in the presence of a group of friends. They grab a sandwich here, a salad there, a yogurt cone there, with a minimum of socializing. And this in turn is a pattern they learned at home. Individual family members eat at different times. Some do most of their eating standing up. And even when people do happen to eat in the same room, they often are watching television or chewing their food while listening to music on their headphones.

This is a major social loss. The family meal is our earliest classroom in civility. It is the best place for our first lessons in manners. When we eat together without distractions, we often talk about important things that are happening in our lives. At the dinner table we even learn how to sit peacefully for a half-hour or so with people we are presently not getting along with very well. If we do not take advantage of the educational opportunities offered by the family meal, we will forever be playing catch-up after that — and not very successfully. I am not privy to any inside information about the dining patterns in the homes of the high school students who have killed their classmates in recent years, but my strong hunch is that the family dinner was not a common occurrence in their lives. I'm not always clear what people mean when they talk about "family values," but here is something that they ought to mean: the family meal is an important training ground for citizenship.

Christians have special reasons to worry about an eating-alone culture. The meal is an important part of our worshiping life. Just before Jesus died, he ate with his disciples, and he told them to keep having that kind of meal together "in remembrance of me." The book of Revelation even tells us that we can expect a major banquet when we get to heaven, "the wedding feast of the Lamb." Church meals — both our formal communion services and our informal potluck suppers — are a good way, then, of getting ready for the afterlife. And family dinners may serve the same function. But even if they don't have that kind of eternal significance, they are certainly important to a healthy culture in the here-and-now.

We are probably safe to let the operators of bowling alleys worry about all the folks who are bowling alone these days. But the habit of eating alone ought to concern us all.

The "Larger Faith"

In the early 1980s, when I was a guest professor at a college in western Pennsylvania, I came across a group of people who had formed a house church whose worship and teaching was loyal to the original Universalist movement in North America. The Universalists had organized as a denomination in 1793 in order to propagate what they saw as a consistent alternative to the classic positions associated with Calvinism and its Arminian opponents regarding the extent of Christ's atoning work. The Arminians insisted that Christ died for everyone but not everyone will be saved, while the Calvinists argued that, since only the elect are to be saved, they are the only ones for whom Christ died. The Universalists insisted that Christ died for everyone and everyone will in the end be saved.

These folks in western Pennsylvania considered themselves to be a faithful remnant of true Universalists. They were distressed by the fact that their denomination's merger with the Unitarians in 1961, to form the Unitarian Universalist Association, had resulted in the loss of their historic identity. On their view, the genius of original Universalism had been overwhelmed by a vague sort of Unitarian spirituality that lacked any solid theological foundation. In one of my conversations with these Pennsylvanians, I told them about what I considered to be a funny piece of theological humor that had made the rounds when the 1961 merger took place: the two different theologies formed an interesting new combination, with the Universalists arguing that God is too good to damn us and the Unitarians insisting that we are too good to be damned. My friends in Pennsylvania did not think that was very funny. For them it was a tragedy that their unique theological perspective had virtually disappeared from the theological scene.

Of course, there are plenty of universalists around these days. But they are not of the "capital-U" variety. Present-day universalism is mostly a vapid inclusivism in which a friendly God is committed to embracing all of his creatures without running the risk of being "judgmental." These folks in Pennsylvania wanted nothing to do with that kind of thinking. They believed that we human beings are hopelessly lost without the atoning work of Christ, but that the sovereign grace that sent Jesus to shed his blood on the Cross was sufficient to atone for all of our sins, including the sin of persistent unbelief.

The small remnant of loyal Universalists in Pennsylvania did not persuade me to embrace their theology. But I have to admit that I found their views intriguing. Recently I did some reading about the history of Universalism. For one of the books that I read, subtitled *A Short History of American Universalism*, the author, Charles Howe, had chosen as his title a phrase that I had heard the folks in Pennsylvania use to describe their perspective: *The Larger Faith*.

I like that notion of having a "larger faith." I once heard a fascinating lecture by the Japanese missiologist Kosuke Koyama, in which he argued that every Christian has to decide whether he or she has a "stingy God" or a "generous God." The God that I read about in the Bible is an overwhelmingly generous Creator and Redeemer. I worry a lot about how evangelicals sometimes try to turn him into a stingy God. We try to contain him within our favorite theological systems and to limit his faithfulness to our favorite projects and causes. He will not be restricted in that manner. "His ways are not our ways."

None of that leads me to embrace any form of universalism. It is precisely God's generosity that keeps him from coercing us into the realm of saving grace. His generosity is displayed most clearly in what he *invites* us to accept.

We serve a Lord to whom all authority in heaven and on earth has been given, a Lord who has promised that someday he will return to "make all things new." There is nothing stingy about this "larger faith."